'A wonderfully clear-headed account of how we can fight both climate change and widening inequality: consumers pay higher prices proportional to their carbon footprints but get the money back in the form of dividends in equal payments to every man, woman, and child. If there's to be a Green New Deal, this is the kind of policy we'll need.'

Robert Reich, former U.S. Secretary of Labor

'Carbon dividends are key to dealing with the threats of a changing climate. Read this book to learn about an important part of the solution to this looming problem.'

George P. Shultz, former U.S. Secretary of State

'Boyce makes clear the one climate policy that would work: 'carbon fee and dividend.' The public will love it - it puts money in their pocket. Young people should demand it, to save their planet and their future.'

James Hansen, former director of the NASA Goddard Institute for Space Studies

'The threat of climate change is real. But action is still too little, too late. This book provides a bold and disruptive idea that could shape the new wave of policy and action on climate change. It would be ambitious, leading the world to drastically cut emissions, and also equitable, ensuring cooperation in action.'

Sunita Narain, Centre for Science and Environment, New Delhi

T0273752

'Congress must act to stop the rising damage and costs of climate change – and that action must be based on sound scientific research. The carbon cap and dividend approach is a simple and fair way to require polluters to pay and put the money into the pockets of American taxpayers. And thanks to Professor Boyce's research, we know just how effective it can be.'

U.S. Senator Chris Van Hollen

'This crisply written book makes a compelling – and highly accessible – case for using carbon pricing to tackle the twin challenges of our time: climate change and income inequality. Covering the science, the markets, and the politics, Boyce argues that a carbon dividend strategy is simple, effective, and fair. Regardless of where one falls in the nuances of the climate policy debate, this is a gem of a volume.'

Manuel Pastor, director of the Program for Environmental and Regional Equity, University of Southern California

'Hooray for James Boyce's The Case for Carbon Dividends. In clear and compelling English, it explains the carbon pollution challenge and makes the case for citizen dividends as a straightforward solution. Too many global warming debates proceed in highly technical terms, leaving regular citizens – rightly – worried that they will pay the price for new taxes and rules. But carbon dividends – equal remittances from carbon tax revenues sent to every American man, woman, and child each year – are easy to understand, impose more costs on rich households that currently use more dirty energy, and would leave most working and middle-class families as net winners. This primer should kick start many community debates, because it tells us exactly

how the United States can make rapid progress toward a green economy and become a more equal democracy in the process.'
Theda Skocpol, Victor S. Thomas Professor of Government and Sociology, Harvard University, and Director of the Scholars Strategy Network

'This is the best thing ever written on the subject. Clear, eloquent and irrefutable, it's a must-read for all concerned with surviving the 21st century.'
Peter Barnes, author of *With Liberty and Dividends for All*

'People fight climate change when they believe in a solution. Boyce's guide to carbon dividends is the indispensable guide for what's big, bold, fair and strong enough for the job. We need this book!'
Camila Thorndike, co-founder, Our Climate

'We define the atmosphere as a common property resource, so we can understand carbon dividends as payments by users of the resource to its owners – this is economic democracy. James Boyce uses principles of equity and economic efficiency to build a practical strategy to address climate change.'
Dallas Burtraw, Darius Gaskins Senior Fellow, Resources for the Future

The Case for
Carbon Dividends

James K. Boyce

———————

The Case for Carbon Dividends

polity

First published in 2019 by Polity Press

Polity Press
65 Bridge Street
Cambridge CB2 1UR, UK

Polity Press
101 Station Landing
Suite 300
Medford, MA 02155, USA

ISBN-13: 978-1-5095-2654-3
ISBN-13: 978-1-5095-2655-0 (pb)

A catalogue record for this book is available from the British Library.

Library of Congress Cataloging-in-Publication Data

Names: Boyce, James K., author.
Title: The case for carbon dividends / James Boyce.
Description: Medford, MA : Polity, 2019. | Series: The case for | Includes
   bibliographical references and index.
Identifiers: LCCN 2018057103 (print) | LCCN 2018061138 (ebook) | ISBN
   9781509526581 (Epub) | ISBN 9781509526543 (hardback) | ISBN 9781509526550
   (paperback)
Subjects: LCSH: Carbon offsetting. | Carbon offsetting--Economic aspects. |
   Carbon offsetting--Law and legislation. | Emissions trading. | Emissions
   trading--Economic aspects. | BISAC: POLITICAL SCIENCE / Public Policy /
   Economic Policy.
Classification: LCC HC79.P55 (ebook) | LCC HC79.P55 B69 2019 (print) | DDC
   363.738/746--dc23
LC record available at https://lccn.loc.gov/2018057103

Typeset in 11 on 15 Sabon by Servis Filmsetting Ltd, Stockport, Cheshire
Printed and bound in the UK By CPI Group (UK) Ltd, Croydon

For further information on Polity, visit our website: politybooks.com

Contents

Figures

Tables

Introduction

To address climate disruption we need insights drawn from science, public policy, and political economy. The key challenge is to curb our use of fossil fuels. The key to cutting fossil-fuel use is to put a price on carbon emissions. And the key to a viable carbon pricing policy, this book argues, is to return carbon revenue to the public as equal per-person dividends.

To succeed, we will need a climate policy that is sustainable politically as well as environmentally. The environmental requirement is widely translated into the target of cutting carbon emissions by at least 80 percent against their 1990 level by the middle of this century. Finding a comparable for-mula for the requirement of political sustainability has been a more elusive goal.

We will need a policy that can secure public

support broad and deep enough to endure for the decades that will be required to complete the clean energy transition. To be this durable, the policy must be capable of winning robust support across the political spectrum.

Past climate policy strategies all too often have started from the premise that cutting our use of fossil fuels will demand sacrifices by the present generation for the sake of future generations. This premise has been shared by climate policy proponents and opponents alike. By failing to craft climate policies that would benefit the majority of people in the present generation – and in the same countries that implement the policy – this "eat your broccoli" narrative has fatally circumscribed the political constituency for climate action.

Carbon price and dividends

A crucial element in climate policy is a carbon price that will raise the cost of fossil fuels and everything produced and distributed by using them. A carbon price can be implemented by means of a tax, a cap-and-permit system, or a combination of the two. In the short run, the carbon price reduces demand for fossil fuels. In the long run, it creates strong incentives for investments in energy efficiency and alternative energy. Carbon pricing faces a major political hurdle, however: how to secure public support for a policy that substantially raises fuel prices for consumers.

This book presents a policy that can meet this challenge: carbon dividends. A price-and-dividend strategy returns the money that consumers pay in higher fossil-fuel prices directly to people in the form of equal payments to every woman, man, and child. The amount that consumers pay in higher prices is proportional to their carbon footprints, so those who consume more fossil fuels pay more. The carbon dividend is paid equally to all, based on the principle of common ownership of our environment – in this case, the environment's limited capacity to absorb carbon emissions safely. Individuals with bigger than average carbon footprints pay more than they get back, while those with smaller than average carbon footprints get back more than they pay.

This is an example of a "feebate" policy: individuals pay fees according to their use of a shared resource and receive rebates by virtue of its common ownership. The concept can be illustrated by means of the following analogy. Imagine that 1,000 people work in an office building whose parking lot has only 300 spaces. If everyone thought they could park for free, the result would be chronic excess demand and congestion. To avert this outcome, a parking fee is charged that constrains demand to fit the lot's capacity. Every month the money collected in parking fees is distributed as equal rebates to everyone who works in the building. Those who take public transport or cycle to work come out well ahead: they pay nothing and get their share of the revenue. Those who carpool to work break more or less even. And those who commute to work every day in a single-occupancy vehicle pay more into the revenue pot than they get back. Carbon dividends apply this idea to parking fossil carbon in the atmosphere.

Because everyone receives the same dividend, regardless of his or her own carbon footprint, all have an incentive to reduce fossil-fuel consumption. Because carbon footprints are correlated with income and expenditure, they are strongly skewed to more affluent households. So the majority of households – including lower-income and middle-class families – come out ahead in simple pocketbook terms, without even counting the policy's environmental benefits.

Carbon dividends, deposited monthly or quarterly into individual accounts, would be a highly transparent way to distribute carbon revenue. A price-and-dividend policy would be revenue-neutral, bypassing paralyzing debates about the optimal size of government. And, because everyone pays according to their use of the scarce resource and receives dividends based on its shared ownership, the policy would be widely perceived as fair.

It is hard to imagine any other climate policy that could secure and sustain broad-based public support in the face of significant escalation in the price of fossil fuels.

This book

The Case for Carbon Dividends offers a succinct explanation of why we need carbon dividends and how they would work. The book consists of four chapters followed by answers to some frequently asked questions.

Chapter 1 makes the case for curtailing our use of fossil fuels. The case rests first and foremost on the role of carbon emissions in driving climate disruption. But there are other compelling reasons to cut carbon, too: to improve air quality and public health and to spur employment-intensive green growth. These benefit the present generation within the same countries that cut their emissions, providing gains in the here and now that, along with carbon dividends, can help surmount the short-sightedness and international cooperation obstacles that have impeded effective climate action.

Chapter 2 lays out the case for carbon pricing. First, I discuss why this is a vital element in the policy mix; while it is not a substitute for regulation and public investment, it is a necessary complement to them. Second, I outline how a carbon price can be put in place by means of either a cap or a tax, or by a policy that combines the attractive features of both. Third, I discuss why carbon pricing is best implemented by means of an upstream system in which the price is charged where fossil fuels first enter the economy.

Chapter 3 highlights an important consequence of any policy that restricts the supply of fossil fuels: their price rises, and the increased prices are passed through to the end-users of fossil fuels and everything produced and distributed using them. This is a feature of the policy, not a bug: the price signal leads to reduced use of fossil fuels economywide. Upper-income households pay more in absolute terms than lower-income households, but as a percentage of their incomes the poor often are hit harder than the affluent. This extra money paid by consumers does not vanish into thin air, however. It winds up somewhere, and the key question is where.

Chapter 4 makes the case for distributing most or all of the carbon revenue to the public as equal per-person dividends. Dividends offset the regressive impact of carbon pricing, turning it into a progressive policy in its impact on income distribution. Like universal basic income, carbon dividends would help to mitigate the problem of wide and rising income inequality. At the same time, universal dividends can help to foster an ethic of shared interests and shared responsibilities in an era when divisiveness is emerging as a peril to pluralist societies.

To illustrate the distributional impacts of carbon prices and dividends, the book focuses on the United States, which among advanced industrialized countries is both the largest emitter of carbon and the hardest nut to crack politically. But the basic finding applies worldwide. In every country, a carbon price-and-dividend policy that devotes a substantial share of the carbon revenue to equal per-person dividends would have a positive net effect on the incomes of the majority of its people, including the poor and the middle class. Furthermore, these income gains accrue regardless of whether or not other countries institute comparable policies. For this reason, national price-and-dividend policies can provide a stepping stone to an international climate accord rather than making national climate policy dependent on international agreements.

The case for carbon dividends, in short, is that they are the most effective and equitable way to confront the greatest environmental challenge of our time.

1

Why Cut Carbon?

The case for a transition to a clean energy future, leaving behind the fossil fuels that powered the world economy from the time of the industrial revolution, above all rests on our duty to safeguard the Earth for future generations. The prevention of "dangerous anthropogenic interference in the climate system," as this goal is inscribed in international law by the United Nations Framework Convention on Climate Change, will require dramatic cuts in carbon dioxide emissions from fossil fuels.

There are three other compelling reasons for us to relegate fossil fuels to history's dustbin. First, air pollution from fossil-fuel combustion leads to millions of premature deaths across the world every year. This alone is enough reason to abandon their use as quickly as we can. Second, investment in energy efficiency and renewable energy technologies can play a key role in the twenty-first-century economy, creating new jobs and new prosperity. Finally, if we introduce carbon dividends as an integral part of the clean energy policy mix, we will give practical expression to the ethical principle that the gifts of nature belong to everyone in equal and common measure.

What science tells us about climate change

Fifty million years ago, the Earth was much hotter than it is today. Crocodiles lived at the North Pole. Ferns grew in Antarctica. Carbon dioxide (CO_2) spewed into the atmosphere by volcanic eruptions blanketed the planet, trapping the sun's heat and pushing polar temperatures close to what we now consider tropical and sub-tropical climates.[1] In the eons since then, plants pulled CO_2 out of the atmosphere, sequestering vast amounts of carbon under the Earth's surface in the form of fossil fuels, and the planet cooled.

Today we are pumping this CO_2 back into the atmosphere at a rate of more than 1,000 tons per second. The climate is gradually warming as a result, and unless we change course soon the warming will not only continue but accelerate. There is a long way to go before we would return to the hothouse planet of 50 million years ago. But scientists forecast that we are on track to see an increase in average temperatures of 3.5°C or more above the pre-industrial level by the end of the present century. The last time the Earth was that hot was in the mid-Pliocene epoch, about 3 million years ago.[2]

Such a scenario would have profoundly unpleasant consequences for humans and other living things. Among others, rising sea levels resulting from the melting of ice sheets and the thermal expansion of the water in the oceans will affect coastal cities worldwide.[3] The frequency and intensity of extreme weather events, including hurricanes and heatwaves, will increase. Ocean acidification, resulting from about a quarter of the CO_2 we emit into the atmosphere being absorbed by seawater, will kill coral reefs and have devastating effects on marine ecosystems.[4] These outcomes are predictable, but they are not inevitable.

The impact of putting vast quantities of fossil carbon back into the atmosphere is often called "global warming." While this is accurate as a description of the average impact on surface temperatures worldwide, it is misleading as a description of impacts in all times and places. In some places, including the east coast of the United States, where I live, we can expect to see increases in the frequency and intensity of extreme winter storms.[5] Some prefer to use the term "climate change" for this reason. Although this, too, is an accurate description, it is open to the objection that the Earth's climate has always been changing. What is distinctive about the current situation is the extraordinary speed at which we are changing the climate.[6] A better label for what's happening is "climate disruption." (In this book I use this interchangeably with the more popular term, "climate change.")

Of course, predictions about the future are always subject to some degree of uncertainty. We do not know exactly how much CO_2 or other greenhouse gases we will emit in coming years. We do not know exactly how much temperatures will change as a result of a given quantity of emissions or exactly what impacts these changes will have on human societies and nature's ecosystems. What we do know, however, is that, unless we move quickly to curb emissions, we – and, even more so, our children and grandchildren – are going to be in for some very nasty experiences.

The good news is that we can act now to avert the worst outcomes. The bad news is that we aren't acting fast enough.

Drawing by Arpita Biswas

Why Cut Carbon?

Responses to climate disruption

Reactions to the threat posed by climate disruption have varied widely. At one end of the spectrum we find outright denial, a stance encapsulated in a tweet by US President Donald Trump claiming that global warming is "bullshit."[7] At the other end we find fears of the end of the world, exemplified in the dire warning by the late cosmologist Stephen Hawking that humans have only a hundred years to move to a new planet.[8]

These opposing reactions are founded on radically divergent understandings of the relationship between humans and nature. Since ancient times some people have seen nature as a stage to be dominated by man (gender-neutral language is not necessary here), transformed according to his desires and will. Others have held that there is an intrinsic "balance of nature" that we can alter only at our peril.

Between complete denial and complete despair, and between hubris and stasis, there is a large middle ground where more realistic appraisals of climate change and the relationship between human activities and the natural world can be found. One can acknowledge the ever-present reality of ecological change without concluding that this means anything goes. And one need not be a doomsayer to conclude that we must move quickly to build a clean energy economy.

Can humans adapt to a radically altered climate? Surely we can. Humans already have adapted to some of the most difficult environments on the planet, from deserts and tropical forests to the Arctic tundra. Some animals and plants will adapt, too, especially with our help; others will not and will go extinct.

Will such accommodation be difficult and painful? Surely it will. The costs of protecting coastal cities (or abandoning those that cannot be protected) alone would be enormous. The death of coral reefs will have profound impacts on fisheries, apart from the loss of their great beauty – a value in its own right. Relocating agriculture in response to changing temperatures and rainfall patterns will be neither smooth nor costless. And because the resources for adaptation will pale beside the needs, they will be rationed by markets and government decisions alike in favor of people and places with the most economic and political power, leaving many to suffer their fates.

To avoid such a future and our vilification by generations to come, the single most important thing we can do today is to reduce our use of fossil fuels sharply and quickly. Carbon dioxide from fossil-fuel combustion today accounts for more than 60 percent of "CO_2-equivalent" greenhouse gas emissions worldwide. Adding methane emissions from fossil fuels, their total contribution is close to two-thirds.[9] The fossil-fuel share of the nation's greenhouse gas emissions is even higher in the US, at 80 percent.[10]

There are other things we can do apart from cutting our use of fossil fuels. We can change land-use practices to reduce carbon emissions and to increase carbon sequestration, and we can invest in R&D on other "negative emissions" technologies.[11] We can curb emissions of other, less important greenhouse gases. But, above all else, we must end the primitive practice of extracting poisonous stuff from under the ground and burning it for our energy.

Fossil fuels are deadly here and now, too

Burning fossil fuels releases many air pollutants, in addition to carbon dioxide, that harm human health, including particulates, sulfur dioxide, nitrogen oxides, and carbon monoxide. The World Health Organization (WHO) calculates that outdoor air pollution was responsible for roughly 3

Why Cut Carbon?

Table 1: Premature deaths from outdoor air pollution (2012)

	Premature deaths	Death rate (per 100,000)
China	1,033,000	76
India	621,000	49
Russia	141,000	98
Indonesia	62,000	25
Pakistan	59,000	33
Ukraine	55,000	120
Nigeria	47,000	28
Egypt	44,000	51
United States	38,000	12
Bangladesh	37,000	24
Turkey	34,000	44
Japan	31,000	24

Note: Premature deaths are rounded to nearest thousand.
Source: World Health Organization, *Ambient Air Pollution: A Global Assessment of Exposure and Burden of Disease*. Geneva: WHO, 2016, Annex 2.

Air pollution is a leading cause of premature mortality around the world. In terms of sheer numbers, China and India have the most deaths. As a percentage of the population, death rates are highest in Ukraine, Russia, and other Eastern European countries. But even in advanced industrialized countries such as the United States and Japan, dirty air kills tens of thousands every year.

million premature deaths in 2012, more than 1 million of which occurred in China (see table 1). The highest mortality rates as a percentage of the population were experienced in Eastern Europe. Ukraine topped the list, as each year more than one in a thousand residents died from outdoor air pollution.

But dirty air is a major killer even in high-income countries, causing 38,000 annual deaths in the US, 26,000 in Germany, and 16,000 in the UK.[12]

The Organisation for Economic Co-operation and Development (OECD) puts the human health cost of outdoor air pollution at more than $500 billion a year in the US, more than $200 billion a year in Japan, and more than $1.7 trillion a year in its thirty-five member states combined.[13]

The outdoor air pollution that harms public health comes not only from burning fossil fuels but also from other sources, including wildfires, burning of biomass, and ammonia releases from fertilizer and livestock. But the carbonaceous particles released in fossil-fuel combustion are especially hazardous. Road transportation alone is estimated to account for about half the mortality from outdoor air pollution in the European Union.[14] In the United States, land transport, electricity generation, and residential energy use are estimated to account for about two-thirds.[15]

The health damages from fossil-fuel pollutants, which along with the climate damages from CO_2 emissions constitute what has been called the "Social Cost of Atmospheric Release," provide another compelling reason to move as quickly as possible in the transition to clean energy.[16] The desire to improve air quality helps to explain why China has moved more aggressively in recent years to reduce its use of fossil fuels.[17] Similarly, a study for the Netherlands Environmental Assessment Agency concluded that the air quality benefits from a stringent climate policy in the European Union would be more than enough to offset the policy's costs, "even when the long-term benefits of avoided climate impacts are not taken into account."[18]

Politically, the health costs of air pollution are especially salient because they are incurred by people who are alive today in the same locations where the fossil-fuel emissions occur. In this respect they differ from the effects of climate change that will be further away in time and space. The air-quality benefits of cutting fossil-fuel use can help surmount the obstacles to climate policy posed by short-term time horizons and the "free rider" problem that impedes concerted international action.

In the 2015 Paris Agreement, the nations of the world agreed on the goal of limiting the average rise in global temperatures to between 1.5 and 2°C. It is estimated that attainment of this goal would prevent 150 million premature deaths from air pollution between now and the end of the century. Many of these averted deaths would be in the cities of Asia and Africa: 4 million in Delhi, for example, 3.6 million in Dhaka, 1.4 million in Lagos, and 930,000 in Guangzhou. But lives would be saved throughout the world, including an estimated 290,000 in Mexico City, 130,000 in Los Angeles, and 53,000 in London.[19]

In short, saving lives here and now is another powerful reason to cut carbon.

Residents of Delhi, India, suffer from some of the world's worst air pollution, much of it caused by the use of fossil fuels.

Why Cut Carbon?

Clean energy and the green economy

On top of the environmental benefits from a stable climate and cleaner air, the energy revolution of the twenty-first century will bring substantial economic payoffs. Investment in energy efficiency and renewable energy creates more jobs than the same amount of investment in the fossil-fuel industry. Policies to guarantee a just transition can protect workers and local economies that have been dependent on fossil-fuel extraction. New energy technologies can also strengthen the resilience of economies against infrastructure failures caused by natural or man-made disasters.

The job creation benefits are illustrated in table 2, which compares the employment generated by clean energy investments to those in fossil-fuel production in four major economies around the world. Clean energy investments here include spending on energy efficiency (such as building retrofits and mass transit) as well as renewable energy sources (solar power, wind power, and clean biomass).[20]

The first two columns in table 2 show jobs per million dollars of investment. These vary across countries, reflecting differences in labor costs and labor intensity, but in all four countries the number

Table 2: Job gains from investing in clean energy

| | Jobs per $1 million investment | | Net gains from investing 1.5% of GDP in clean energy | |
	Clean energy	Fossil fuels	Jobs	Share of labor force
Brazil	37.1	21.2	395,000	0.4%
China	133.1	74.4	6,400,000	0.6%
South Africa	70.6	33.1	126,000	0.7%
United States	8.7	3.7	650,000	0.5%

Source: Robert Pollin, *Greening the Global Economy,* Cambridge, MA: MIT Press, 2015, tables 6.1 and 6.2.

The clean energy transition will create more jobs than it will destroy. Investments in energy efficiency and alternative energy are more labor-intensive and have a higher share of domestic labor than investments in fossil fuels.

of jobs per clean energy dollar is roughly double the number per dollar invested in the fossil-fuels sector. This is because clean energy investments are more labor-intensive. For countries that import fossil fuels, clean energy also creates jobs at home rather than abroad. The other two columns show net job gains – the jobs created in clean energy minus the jobs lost in fossil-fuel production – that would occur if each country invested about 1.5 percent of its GDP in clean energy. The gains are equivalent to between 0.4 and 0.7 percent of total employment. In other words, the clean energy investment program would lower national unemployment rates by these amounts.

Investing about 1.5 percent of world GDP in clean energy – in total, about $1.5 trillion a year – is what Robert Pollin and his colleagues at the University of Massachusetts Amherst reckon will be needed to cut fossil-fuel use by 35 percent over the next twenty years. While 1.5 percent sounds modest, this would represent roughly a tripling of current clean energy spending worldwide. Is it a realistic possibility to fund this level of spending?

Today the world devotes more than 2 percent of GDP to military expenditures, spending aimed to protect nations from each other. Spending nearly as much to protect ourselves from the consequences of climate destabilization and air pollution does not seem like an utterly outrageous idea.

In the United States, if we were to spend 1.5 percent of GDP on the clean energy transition, this would be less than half of what we now spend on the military, about the same as what we now spend on alcohol and tobacco, and about ten times what we now spend on pet food. The magnitude is not negligible, but neither is it unthinkable.

The job losses that would be experienced by fossil-fuel workers and their communities cannot be brushed aside by assurances that the economy as a whole will see net gains in employment. New jobs are not automatically filled by those who lose old ones. From a political standpoint, moreover, the workers whose jobs are at risk know who they are, unlike those who will get new jobs that do not yet exist. For both reasons, explicit policies will be necessary to safeguard the livelihoods of those whose jobs disappear. The late trade unionist Tony Mazzocchi put it well: "Those who work with toxic materials on a daily basis, who face the ever-present threat of death from explosions and fires, in order to provide the world with the energy and the materials it needs, deserve a helping hand to make a new start in life."[21]

The financial costs of what Mazzocchi termed a "just transition" are paltry compared to the total investment needed for the clean energy transition. In the US, the cost of guaranteeing re-employment, meeting pension commitments, and assisting communities would be about $500 million per year, less than 1 percent of the total investment bill.[22] The European Parliament voted in 2017 to put some of the revenues from the EU Emissions Trading System into a Just Transition Fund for displaced coal miners in Eastern and Central European member states. In practice, much of the cost of ensuring a just transition can be met simply by redirecting the subsidies governments currently provide to the fossil-fuel industry.[23]

The clean energy transition itself can provide some re-employment opportunities. In the US state of Wyoming, coal miners hit by workforce reductions have found new jobs in the rapidly growing wind power sector.[24] In Germany, the old coal-mining heartland in the Ruhr Valley has become a major supplier of renewable energy and energy efficiency technologies.[25] Another potential sector for re-employment is the restoration of landscapes that were degraded in the past by fossil-fuel extraction. In the US, the "restoration economy" already employs about 126,000 workers – more than twice the number who work in coal mining.[26]

The clean energy transition also creates an opportunity to shift away from concentrated power plants to more distributed networks for power generation, increasing the resilience of electricity grids against disruptive events.[27] Storm-related power outages today cost the US between $20 and $55 billion per year, and the damages are likely to increase with climate disruption.[28] Centralized power systems are vulnerable to cascading failures, as witnessed when Hurricane Sandy struck New York and New Jersey in 2012 and when Hurricane Maria hit Puerto Rico in 2017. Microgrids powered by renewable

Why Cut Carbon?

There is more than one good reason to keep fossil fuels in the ground.

energy, coupled with advanced storage systems and inverters, can be easily decoupled from larger grids ("islanded" in power-sector parlance) in the event of power outages, supplying enough electricity to meet critical needs.[29]

Against these benefits, some economists maintain that carbon pricing policies could dampen economic growth in the long run. They reason that higher fuel prices would lower real wages, diminishing incentives to work and translating into lower GDP. This logic is based on "supply-side" economics which assumes, unrealistically, that the economy typically operates at full employment – that is, with no excess supply of labor – so that anything that reduces the supply of labor automatically reduces GDP. Even so, the estimated impact is quite small. One recent study predicted, for example, that a $50 per ton carbon tax coupled with carbon dividends would cause the US GDP in fifty years to be 0.4 percent lower than otherwise would be the case.[30] To put this in perspective, if the economy continues to grow at 1.4 percent per year, the historically sluggish rate of the past decade, the US GDP will double by that time to be 100 percent higher than that of today. In the long run, in other words, a 0.4 percent haircut looks like a rounding error.

In sum, there are ample reasons why we should cut carbon: to stabilize the Earth's climate for future generations, to avert premature deaths from air pollution in the here and now, and to power a green economic renewal in the twenty-first century. The question is how to achieve the clean energy transition most effectively and most equitably.

2

Why a Price on Carbon?

The reason we need a price on carbon emissions is to limit them. To see why, let's return to the parking analogy.

Imagine a city where the parking of automobiles and other vehicles is free of charge and unregulated, where anyone can park wherever and whenever they like at no cost. The convenience of open access to parking would soon pale in comparison to the resulting mess. With no price incentive to conserve use of the city's limited space for parking, congestion would make it harder and harder to find a spot. With no rules to designate where and when parking is allowed, roads and driveways would be obstructed, street cleaning would be disrupted, and blocked-in vehicles would be common.

To avert this chaotic outcome, we install parking meters along streets and we build parking lots that charge fees. We also enact rules requiring drivers to park between the lines in designated spaces, to reserve spaces for people with disabilities, not to block driveways and fire hydrants, and so on. These solutions are not rocket science. They are common-sense policies, widely implemented by responsible governments for the common good.

The fact that parking in metered spaces along roadsides now has a price does not mean that the city streets have been turned into a commodity. Nor does the fact that there are parking rules mean that residents are less free to move about the city; in fact, it means that they can move more freely. Prices and rules simply mean that the city's limited space to park vehicles cannot be used and abused as an open-access resource.

The same logic applies to parking carbon in the atmosphere.

The case for full-cost pricing

The market prices that we pay today for fossil fuels do not reflect the costs of climate destabilization and air pollution. These costs are what economists call "externalities" – impacts of market transactions on people apart from the buyer or seller. As a result, fossil fuels appear to be cheaper – a lot cheaper – than they really are. Faced with the misleading price signal, consumers, firms, and governments all use more fossil fuels than would be the case if the prices signaled their full cost.

Prices aren't everything. But in real-world economies they are important determinants of what does and doesn't happen. Rules and regulations can affect economic behavior, too, and can help to promote the clean energy transition. But, in the absence of an effective carbon price, regulations resemble a dam on a river: it can check the flow, but the water always wants to go downhill – just as money wants to flow toward the cheapest sources of energy. Carbon pricing levels the terrain.

A carbon price increases prices of fossil fuels – and of everything produced and distributed by using them – in proportion to the carbon dioxide released when the fuels are burned. The higher the price, the less people will consume. As the price of transportation fuel rises, for example, motorists have an incentive to drive less, buy more fuel-efficient vehicles, and demand better public transport. As the price of fossil-fueled electricity goes up, they have an incentive to turn off the lights when they leave the room, buy more efficient appliances, and install solar panels.

Why a Price on Carbon?

In the longer run, a carbon price encourages innovations that further reduce our need for fossil fuels by bending the cost curves for energy efficiency and clean energy. Even the very modest carbon prices in the European Union's Emissions Trading System (EU ETS) have been found to have spurred more patenting of low-carbon technologies.[1] Exactly how much innovation will accelerate in response to any given carbon price cannot be known in advance, but we know that the higher the price, the bigger the boost.

The case for full-cost pricing rests squarely on the signaling function that prices play in decisions on investment and consumption. In this respect, carbon pricing is different from taxation motivated by the need for government revenue. Public investment has a very important role to play in the clean energy transition, but it need not be financed by carbon pricing and usually is not.[2] In most economies, the private sector accounts for most investment, and here the carbon price signal plays a crucial role in redirecting investment away from fossil fuels and into clean energy and energy efficiency.

Why a Price on Carbon?

Carbon pricing today

The good news is that carbon pricing systems now cover about 20 percent of global fossil carbon emissions, a figure that will rise to around 30 percent once China fully implements its national emissions trading system.[3] The bad news is that, even then, 70 percent of world emissions still won't be priced.

When we look at the actually existing carbon prices, the bad news gets worse. Most carbon prices are too low to bring us close to meeting the Paris Agreement's goal of holding the increase in global average temperatures to between 1.5 and 2°C above pre-industrial levels.

Carbon prices are most often expressed in terms of US dollars per metric ton (mt) of CO_2. A convenient way to convert this into more familiar units is to know that \$1/mt CO_2 is roughly equivalent to 43 US cents on a barrel of oil, 1 US cent on a gallon of gasoline, and three-tenths of a euro cent on a litre of petrol. For about three-quarters of the emissions that are covered today by carbon pricing, the price is less than \$10/mt CO_2. The price adds less than 10 cents to the price of a gallon of gasoline and less than 3 euro cents to the price of a litre of petrol. This impact is swamped by ordinary market price fluctuations, as shown in figure 1. It would be delu-

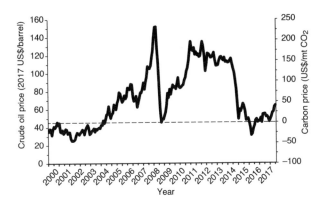

Figure 1 Crude oil prices, 2000–2017 (in constant 2017
US dollars)
**Most existing carbon prices are dwarfed by market
fluctuations in fossil fuel prices.** The figure's right-hand
axis shows a carbon price set to zero at the average
crude oil price in 2017 as a way of gauging the impact
of carbon prices. For example, a carbon price of
US$230/mt CO_2 would be needed to lift the crude oil
price to its level at the market peak in July 2008.

Source: James K. Boyce, "Carbon pricing: effectiveness and equity,"
Ecological Economics 150 (2018).

sional to imagine that carbon prices this low will
suffice to propel the transition from fossil fuels to a
clean energy economy.

Why are existing prices so low? Part of the explanation is the political clout wielded by those with
a vested interest in continued use of fossil fuels –

which also helps to explain why most emissions are not priced at all. Indeed, many countries go so far as to *subsidize* fossil fuels by means of policies that are tantamount to a negative carbon price. A recent IMF study reports that, as of 2015, direct fossil-fuel subsidies amounted to $333 billion a year worldwide.[4] This is equivalent to about $10/mt CO_2 – roughly five times higher than the world's average global carbon price (including unpriced emissions) of $2/mt CO_2.[5] In other words, the average carbon price in the world today is *minus* $8.

A second impediment to higher carbon prices is that politicians and policy-makers fear that they would provoke a backlash from the public. A telling example came in the 2008 US presidential campaign when candidates Hillary Clinton and John McCain, both avowed backers of carbon cap-and-trade legislation, called for a moratorium on the federal gasoline tax (about 18 cents a gallon) to bring relief, as Clinton put it, to "hard-pressed Americans who are trying to pay their gas bills."[6] Yet, compared to the prices that will be needed to cut fossil-fuel use enough to protect the stability of the Earth's climate, 18 cents rounds off to zero.

The risk of a public backlash against higher carbon prices is not unique to the United States, as evidenced by the "yellow vest" protests that broke out in France in November 2018 when the government announced increased taxes on gasoline and diesel. The rationale for the tax hikes – about 12 US cents on a gallon of gasoline and 35 US cents on a gallon of diesel – was to combat climate change by promoting fuel efficiency. The protesters complained that government "talks about the end of the world, while we are talking about the end of the month."[7]

Setting the price

If current carbon prices are too low, what price is "right"? One way to answer this question – the way favored by many but not all economists – is to come up with a monetary estimate of the climate damage per ton of carbon emissions, something called the "social cost of carbon" (SCC). On this basis, the economist prescribes the "optimal" carbon price and the "efficient" level of emissions reduction. For example, if the SCC is reckoned to be $100/mt CO_2, that's the right price, and however much emissions are reduced as a result is the right amount.

An alternative way to decide on the right price is to ask how much more carbon we can safely release into the atmosphere and still prevent what the

Why a Price on Carbon?

United Nations Framework Convention on Climate Change (UNFCCC) calls "dangerous anthropogenic interference with the climate system." This sets a limit on how much more fossil carbon we can burn – ever – an amount that can be rationed over future years during the clean energy transition. The criterion for setting the quantity of emissions and the associated carbon price here is safety as defined by scientists, not efficiency as defined by economists.

In the hands of mainstream economists, the efficiency criterion often yields much lower recommended prices than the safety criterion and much bigger increases in global temperatures. The difference is illustrated in figure 2, which contrasts two prescriptions for the carbon price trajectory. The lower line shows the "efficient" carbon price prescribed by a leading economic model. Starting at about $37/mt CO_2 in 2020, it rises to about $100 in 2050. The upper line shows the price that would be needed, according to the same model, to hold the increase in average global temperatures to 2.5°C. It starts at about $230/mt CO_2 in 2020 and rises to about $1,000 by the middle of this century. The first price trajectory would add about $1 (in today's money) to the price of a gallon of gasoline in 2050; the second would add more than $8. Meeting the

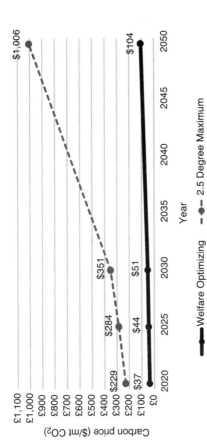

Figure 2 Carbon price paths
The carbon price needed to limit the rise in global temperature to 2.5°C is far higher than the "optimal" social cost of carbon typically prescribed by economic models that claim to weigh benefits against costs. The global CO_2 price is here expressed in constant 2010 US dollars.

Source: Based on data in William D. Nordhaus, "Revisiting the social cost of carbon," *Proceedings of the National Academy of Sciences* 114/7 (2017), table 1.

Paris goal of holding the increase to between 1.5 and 2°C could require even higher prices.

Under the so-called efficient trajectory, average global temperatures at the turn of the century would be 3.5°C (6.3°F) above pre-industrial levels and continue to rise in the twenty-second century. This is below the 4°C increase by 2100 in the model's "business as usual" scenario with no carbon price, but still hot enough to return the Earth to the temperature conditions last experienced more than 3 million years ago in the mid-Pliocene epoch. There were large geographical variations in the extent of warming then as compared to now, with the difference being about three times greater at high northern latitudes. Global sea level was at least 6 metres higher than today, and possibly 20 metres higher.[8]

To put this time scale in perspective, *Homo sapiens* evolved about 200,000 years ago. Agriculture originated a mere 10,000 years ago. Translating the passage of geological time into the span of a single year, if we were to reckon that the Pliocene occurred in January, humans evolved in early December, agriculture began on December 31st, and it would ostensibly be efficient to reset global temperatures to the Pliocene level in the last 15 minutes of the year.

Why a Price on Carbon?

The "social cost of carbon"

How do mainstream economists manage to contemplate such a radical change with seeming equanimity? Their prescriptions rest on assumptions that are built into the code of their models. These include damage functions that predict the extent of economic losses that would result from a given change in temperature. Extrapolating from past experience into uncharted territory is always problematic, even when past data are readily available. In the case of impacts for which data are not available – such as extreme sea-level rise, ocean acidification, biodiversity loss, and the risk of catastrophic events – extrapolation is impossible, and so damages are calculated by rules of thumb. In the model from which figure 2 is derived, these big unknowns are accounted for simply by adding 25 percent to other estimated costs.[9]

The models then convert the magnitude of future damages into present values by means of a "discount rate" that makes a dollar of future pain worth less than a dollar of present gain. The rationale is that we use this logic in individual decisions: we would rather have a dollar today than the same dollar (with the same purchasing power, adjusted for inflation) tomorrow. Economists can calculate a person's discount rate by asking how much she would be willing to pay today to receive a certain sum of money one year, two years, or fifty years from now.

In applying discount rates to climate change, economists assume that the same logic that individual mortals use in personal decisions about the future is appropriate for social decisions that will impact the well-being of future generations. At figure 2's preferred discount rate of 4¼ percent, for example, $1 million in damages (in today's money) one century from now counts for only $15,000 today. Two centuries from now the same damages count for only $250.[10] It would be "inefficient" if those of us alive today were to spend more than this to avert imposing these costs on future generations. Discounting melts away future costs as inexorably as climate change is melting the polar ice sheets.

These and other assumptions in economic models can produce some eye-popping conclusions. In this particular model, which yields SCC estimates that lie in the middle range of those produced by other models, a whopping 6°C warming would merely shave 8.5 percent off future global incomes. This may seem like a rather modest estimate of the cost from cooking the planet to temperatures last seen not 3 million but about 15 million years ago.

Such a cost looks even more tolerable when the models assume that, if we do nothing to arrest climate change, average incomes will nevertheless quadruple or more in the coming century.[11] "While there are plausible reasons to act quickly on climate change," remarks the Yale economist and recent Nobel laureate William Nordhaus, whose model produced the results in figure 2, "the need to redistribute income to a wealthy future does not seem to be one of them."[12]

Commenting on how economic models estimate the costs of climate change, the Intergovernmental Panel on Climate Change (IPCC) offers the following diplomatically worded verdict: "These impact assessments are incomplete and depend on a large number of assumptions, many of which are disputable."[13] The MIT economist Robert Pindyck is more blunt: "The models are so deeply flawed as to be close to useless as tools for policy analysis. Worse yet, their use suggests a level of knowledge and precision that is simply illusory, and can be highly misleading."[14]

Despite these defects, the SCC plays an important role in policy-making. In the US, for example, a presidential executive order requires cost–benefit analysis for all major proposed environmental regulations. In the case of climate policy, the SCC is used for this purpose. An Interagency Working Group on the Social Cost of Carbon, established in 2010 to come up with an official number, chose a central value of $42/mt CO_2 as the SCC for 2020, close to the "optimal" price given by the lower line in figure 2.[15] Federal regulations could not require spending more than this to curb emissions.

Of course, different assumptions generate higher or lower SCCs. The Stern Review, a study commissioned by the UK government and published in 2007, used a considerably lower discount rate and recommended a much higher SCC that would lead to steeper cuts in emissions.[16] The opposite occurred in 2017, when the Trump administration disbanded the working group and proposed to repeal the Clean Power Plan, an Obama-era policy that would have slashed emissions from coal-burning plants. In its new regulatory impact analysis, Trump's Environmental Protection Agency upped the discount rate and zeroed out all benefits from climate change mitigation that would accrue outside the US to arrive at new SCC of only $1-6/mt CO_2 – a price that would add no more than 6 cents to the price of a gallon of gasoline.[17]

Why a Price on Carbon?

Target-based carbon prices

A very different way to set the right carbon price is to anchor it to a fixed target, such as the 1.5 to 2°C warming limit of the Paris Agreement, and let the target drive the price. This can be done via either a cap-and-permit system or a carbon tax indexed to emission reductions, as described below. In this case, the criterion for choosing the right level of emissions and the right carbon price is safety, not efficiency as in the economists' SCC.

Safety is the foundation for many environmental policies. In the US, for example, the Clean Air Act mandates the Environmental Protection Agency to set air quality standards for "the protection of public health and welfare," allowing "an adequate margin of safety" – not to choose the "efficient" level of air pollution by weighing the benefits of protecting health against its cost. In its historic 2007 decision in the case *Massachusetts et al.* v. *Environmental Protection Agency*, the Supreme Court ruled that the Clean Air Act gives the federal government authority to regulate greenhouse gas emissions. The legal basis for US climate policy therefore is safety.

A similar logic led the UK government to drop the SCC in 2009 in favor of "a target-consistent approach, based on estimates of the abatement costs that will need to be incurred to meet specific emissions reduction targets."[18] Likewise, the 2017 report of the High-Level Commission on Carbon Prices, co-chaired by the economists Nicholas Stern and Joseph Stiglitz, concluded that the social costs of carbon in many modeling exercises "probably underestimate these costs by a very large margin" and instead focused on carbon price trajectories consistent with the Paris Agreement's temperature objective.[19] In this approach, the emissions reduction target is set by what is considered safe and the carbon price is determined by the cost of meeting it.

Of course, choosing the target is not a straightforward matter, and there is always some degree of arbitrariness in deciding what is "safe." In 2012, the UNFCCC endorsed a target of 2°C warming.[20] After this, dozens of nations led by the Alliance of Small Island States and the least-developed countries continued to urge a more stringent 1.5°C target. The Paris Agreement represented a compromise, defining the goal as "holding the increase in the global average temperature to well below 2°C above pre-industrial levels and pursuing efforts to limit the temperature increase to 1.5°C."[21] While this may not be a perfect target, climate scientists have accepted it as "an easily understood, politically useful marker to communicate the urgency of the climate change problem and to drive action on a global scale."[22]

Carbon caps versus carbon taxes

There are two ways to put a price on carbon: a cap-and-permit system and a carbon tax:

- A cap-and permit system sets a limit (cap) on the quantity of carbon emissions to be allowed each year and issues permits (one permit = 1 ton of CO_2) up to that limit. The quantity is fixed, while the permit price can vary. If there is an economic boom that stokes demand for fossil fuels, for example, the carbon price will be higher than during a recession.
- A tax sets the carbon price and allows the quantity of emissions to vary. At any fixed price, for example, the quantity of emissions will be higher during a boom than during a recession.

A cap-and-permit system is like a carbon tax with a variable price. A carbon tax is like a permit system with a fixed price.

This difference between the two wouldn't matter

much if we could predict with certainty how emissions will respond to any given carbon price. If we knew this, we could set the price and get the desired quantity, or set the quantity and get the desired price. But in practice our knowledge about the price–quantity relationship is imprecise. We know that a higher tax will result in fewer emissions and that a tighter cap will result in a higher price. But we do not know exact magnitudes, since the relationship will depend, for instance, on whether the economy is in a boom or a slump, and whether technological innovations that lower the costs of energy efficiency and alternative energy come quickly or slowly. These things cannot be fully known in advance.

Insofar as past experience provides a reliable guide, we can expect that substantial increases in fossil-fuel prices will be needed to meet the Paris target. Demand for fossil fuels is fairly inelastic, meaning that the percentage change in quantity is smaller than the percentage change in price. This reflects the fact that energy for most is a necessity, not a luxury: we consume less of it when prices go up, but not a whole lot less.

The ratio between the percentage change in quantity and the percentage change in price is what economists call the "price elasticity of demand." A recent review of hundreds of empirical studies, all published between 1990 and 2016, found an average price elasticity of –0.2 in the short run and –0.6 in the long run.[23] That is, a 10 percent increase in energy prices resulted on average in a 2 percent decline in the quantity consumed in the first year or two and a 6 percent decline a few years later. In the short run, motorists may respond to higher fuel prices by driving less, carpooling, and taking public transport more often (if it is available). In the longer run, they may respond by purchasing more fuel-efficient vehicles or moving to places with shorter commutes. Even in the long run, however, the percentage reduction in demand usually turns out to be smaller than the percentage increase in fuel prices that brought it about.

Elasticities varied considerably from one study to another, reflecting differences across fuels, locations, times, and computation methods. For example, it is easier to cut fossil-fuel use in places with well-developed public transportation than in places where the only alternative to driving an automobile is to stay home. The authors also found that price elasticities in recent time periods tend to be lower than they were in earlier years, suggesting that less expensive ways to cut fuel use were depleted in the wake of past energy crises. The low-hanging fruit is picked first.

Why a Price on Carbon?

Because the precise relationship between carbon prices and emission quantities cannot be known in advance, we can either set the quantity and let the price adjust or set the price and let the quantity adjust. If our main objective is to meet fixed targets for reducing emissions, it makes more sense to set the quantity.

The most straightforward way to do this is to establish a cap on total emissions that declines over time and every year to auction permits up to the limit set by the cap. For example, a policy that would cut emissions by 80 percent against the current level in a thirty-year time frame translates into emission reductions at the rate of roughly 5 percent per year. Each year, the number of permits to be auctioned is given by this tightening cap. The resulting price would vary with demand for permits.

An alternative way to achieve the same result is to implement a carbon tax with a rate that automatically adjusts in response to any gaps between targets and the change in emissions in response to the tax. If and when the emissions reduction does not meet the target, the tax rate (that is, the carbon price) goes up. Switzerland did this when it instituted a CO_2 levy on power plants.[24]

Another option is to combine the two policies, setting a floor price for permits (the tax) and holding permit auctions that trigger higher carbon prices whenever demand at the floor price exceeds the supply (the cap). The floor price improves the predictability of future carbon prices, which may be desirable for planning and investment decisions. At the same time, the cap on the quantity of permits ensures that emission targets are met. (A price ceiling, in contrast, would compromise the emissions reduction objective if and when demand for permits at the ceiling price exceeds the cap.)

The carbon price guarantee

With a target-based carbon price, we do not need to know the unknowable – exactly how the relationship between use of fossil fuels and the carbon price will play out. The policy is guaranteed to hit the emissions target no matter whether the economy goes into a boom or a bust, no matter whether energy efficiency and renewable energy costs fall quickly or slowly, no matter whether demand turns out to be more or less inelastic than it was in the past.

This distinctive feature sets target-based carbon pricing apart from other policies. The overall emissions reduction that will be brought about by fuel economy regulations on automobiles, for example, is uncertain. Although the standards will lead to fewer emissions per mile, total emissions depend on the number of miles traveled. Improvements in fuel efficiency could even have a "rebound effect" if motorists drive more because it costs them less. Similarly, renewable portfolio standards for electric utilities, requiring them to obtain a certain percentage of their power from renewable sources, will lead to lower emissions per kilowatt, but total emissions depend on how much electricity consumers use. While there may be good reasons to include such regulations in the policy mix, there can be no assurance that they will suffice to meet emission reduction targets unless accompanied by a target-based carbon price.[25]

The same can be said of a carbon price that is *not* anchored to quantity targets. We could simply institute a carbon tax and hope for the best, but, unless the tax rate rises automatically when emissions exceed the desired level, there can be no guarantee that the tax will do the job. All one can do is hope for the best.

There is one and only one policy that can ensure that emissions reduction goals are met without fail: setting an absolute limit on the amount of fossil fuels we burn. This restriction in supply causes fossil-fuel prices to rise above what they otherwise would have been. The price of carbon is the result of the difference between fuel prices with and without this limit.

If regulations, public investments, moral suasion, or other policies and efforts prove to be highly effective in curbing our use of fossil fuels, the price resulting from a target-based carbon pricing policy will turn out to be low. Indeed, if these other measures are sufficient to meet the targets on their own, the auction price would fall to zero in the absence of a floor price: emissions reduction targets would be met without the carbon price. If other measures turn out to be insufficient, however, target-based carbon pricing guarantees that the targets nevertheless will be met.

Climate change is not a challenge that can be best addressed by a single policy. Just as we use a combination of policies to combat parking congestion in urban areas, we can use a combination of carbon pricing, smart regulations, and public investment to combat the excessive dumping of carbon into the Earth's atmosphere. In their enthusiasm for one policy or another, proponents sometimes are tempted to dismiss other policies as unnecessary or even undesirable. But good policies can be mutually supportive rather than mutually exclusive. There is

no intrinsic reason for proponents of public investment or regulations to oppose target-based carbon
pricing, if only as an insurance policy in case these
other measures fall short in achieving emission-
reduction goals. Having no insurance when you
need it is far worse than having insurance when you
don't.

Where to charge the price?

A convenient attribute of fossil fuels is that we
don't have to wait until they are actually burned
to know how much carbon dioxide will be emitted
in the process. We know the amount of carbon in
a metric ton of coal, a barrel of oil, and a cubic
foot of natural gas. We know that, when the fuel
is burned, each kilogram of carbon will bond with
oxygen molecules from the air to create 3.67 kg of
carbon dioxide. In this respect, CO_2 differs from
the other pollutants that are released in fossil-fuel
combustion. The amount of sulfur dioxide emitted
by a coal-fired power plant varies, for example,
depending on the source of the coal and the pollution controls in use when it is burned.

This means that, rather than charging the carbon
price where the CO_2 is emitted – collecting the

permits or levying the tax at every smokestack and every tailpipe – the price can be charged "upstream" at the tanker ports, pipeline terminals, and coalmine heads where fossil fuels first enter the economy. In the US, the Congressional Budget Office reckons that an upstream system would require only about 2,000 collection points nationwide.[26] An end-of-pipe system, in contrast, would require emission monitoring and pricing enforcement at millions of sites throughout the economy.

For each ton of CO_2 that will be emitted once the fossil fuel is burned, the firm that brings the fuel into the economy would be required to turn in a permit or pay the tax. This is a one-time charge. It does not license the firm to bring in another ton every year, any more than putting money in a parking meter allows you to park in a spot forever. Each new ton requires a new permit or tax payment.

Existing carbon pricing systems often operate midstream. The price is charged at power plants, large industrial facilities, or fuel distributors – these are the "compliance entities" in bureaucratic parlance – situated between initial suppliers of fossil fuels and final consumers. As long as these entities are few in number, the administrative costs remain tractable. Midstream carbon pricing systems typically cover specific sectors rather than all users of fossil fuels. An upstream system, in contrast, is comprehensive.

Regardless of where the carbon price is charged, it is the final users of fossil fuels and everything produced or distributed using them who ultimately pay it. The upstream or midstream firms where the carbon price is charged pass it on to their customers. The carbon price becomes part of their cost of doing business, increasing the prices of goods and services in proportion to the fossil carbon burned to produce them. When the price of coal goes up, for example, so does the price of coal-fired electricity. Charging the price to coal-fired power plants does not mean that they ultimately foot the bill.

The pass-through of the carbon price to final users is not only predictable but also desirable. It transmits the price signals that tell users it's a good idea to turn off unnecessary lights, invest in insulation and more fuel-efficient vehicles and appliances, and buy goods and services that are produced and distributed by less carbon-intensive means.

This feature of carbon pricing has important implications for its distributional effects and its political sustainability, as we will see in the next chapter.

3

What is Carbon Rent?

In October 1973, war broke out between Israel, Egypt, and Syria. The recently formed Organization of Arab Petroleum Exporting Countries announced an embargo on exports to nations that supported Israel. By January 1974, the world oil price had quadrupled to nearly $12 a barrel, an episode today remembered as the world's first oil shock. Five years later, a second shock was precipitated by the Iranian revolution and the Iran–Iraq war, and the world oil price jumped to about $40 a barrel.

On both occasions, the increase in oil prices greatly exceeded the decrease in supplies. World crude oil production was basically flat in 1973–4, having risen 9 percent the year before; in 1979–80 it fell by only 4 percent.[1] Yet prices soared. The lesson in the economics of oil was clear: when supplies are cut, prices go up. A lot.

What is Carbon Rent?

Keeping fossil fuels in the ground

The central goal of any serious climate policy is to keep fossil fuels in the ground. Yet some climate activists who embrace this and related slogans such as "keep the oil in the soil" are deeply skeptical about policies that would put a price on carbon.

One reasonable basis for skepticism is the fact that, where carbon pricing has been implemented so far, the price typically has been too low to make much of a difference. But this points to the need for higher prices, not a price of zero. It is not a good reason to oppose carbon pricing across the board, any more than having tasted weak coffee is a good reason never to drink coffee again.

Sometimes the skepticism is also a result of muddled thinking. Rather than charging a price, the logic goes, wouldn't it be fairer and more effective just to keep the fossils in the ground, just to "say no" to dumping carbon into the atmosphere? Why should anyone be able to pay to pollute? "The air and water belong to all of us," declares a critic of carbon pricing, "and nobody has the right to despoil it for profit."[2]

In light of this objection it is useful to consider what would happen if we were to succeed in keeping fossil fuels in the ground somewhere big enough

What is Carbon Rent?

Keeping fossil fuels in the ground is the central task of any serious climate policy. The question is: How to do it effectively and equitably?

Created by Angie Vanessa Cárdenas for Oilwatch.

to make a difference. Imagine, for example, that the people of Nigeria somehow force their government and its multinational partners to keep that country's oil in the soil. Imagine, for good measure, that the people of Angola do the same. These are the two biggest oil producers in sub-Saharan Africa, together accounting for about 4 percent of world supply. What would happen to oil prices?

The answer, of course, is that they would go up. Perhaps prices would not rise as much as in

1979–80, or perhaps they would rise even more, especially if the shutdown led to fear that other countries will follow suit. The increase in the price of crude oil would be passed on in higher prices for transportation fuels, heating oil, and all goods and services that use oil in their production and distribution, just as in the case of carbon pricing.

In this case, where would the money – the extra money paid by consumers – ultimately go? It would flow to the oil producers who do *not* keep their oil in the soil. The biggest beneficiaries would be oil companies in Saudi Arabia, Russia, and the United States, the world's top three producers. As the price of oil rises, their profit margins would climb. The net result would be a transfer of money – lots of it – from consumers to some of the richest and most powerful corporations in the world, among them some of the most stubborn opponents of fair and effective climate policies. Oops.

The "just say no" strategy would be effective in reducing emissions, at least until other countries stepped up production to fill the gap in response to rising prices. Likewise, the 1973 oil shock has been credited with giving the world a head start in the fight against climate change.[3] But in terms of who pockets the money from higher fuel prices, few would call the outcome fair.

What is Carbon Rent?

How much money is at stake?

The amount of money on the table is potentially large. Very large. The size of the *carbon rent* – the extra money that is paid by consumers as a result of policies that curb emissions of fossil carbon – will depend on how quickly we curtail the supply of fossil fuels and how much prices rise as a result. To give some idea of the possibilities, table 3 presents two illustrative scenarios for the United States, both of which assume that fossil-fuel use is reduced at a constant rate that yields an 80 percent reduction in thirty years.

The first scenario assumes that a carbon price of $50/mt CO_2 is established in the first year of the policy and then increases at 5 percent per year.[4] In this case, the carbon price rises to about $80/mt CO_2 in the policy's tenth year, enough to add about 65 cents to the price of a gallon of gasoline. Cumulative carbon rent over the decade would amount to $2.4 trillion, equivalent to about $700 per person per year.

The second scenario extrapolates from how fossil-fuel prices responded to changes in supply in the past few decades. To achieve emission reductions of 5.22 percent per year (this is the constant rate required to bring about an 80 percent total cut

What is Carbon Rent?

Table 3: Carbon rent: two scenarios

	Scenario 1	Scenario 2
CO_2 price in year 1	$50/mt	$32/mt
CO_2 price in year 10	$80/mt	$485/mt
Cumulative revenue, years 1–10	$2.4 trillion	$8.2 trillion
Average revenue per person per year	$700	$2,400

Note: Constant dollars (today's money, excluding effects of inflation).
Sources: Author's calculations based on initial fossil-fuel price of $3 per gallon of gasoline and initial fossil CO_2 emissions of 5,143 million metric tons (the 2017 level). Quantity of US emissions in 2017 from US Energy Information Administration: www.eia.gov/todayinenergy/detail.php?id=34872. Fossil CO_2 emissions per gallon of E10 gasoline from US Energy Information Administration: www.eia.gov/tools/faqs/faq.php?id=307&t=11. Population projections from US Census Bureau: www.census.gov/data/tables/2017/demo/popproj/2017-summary-tables.html.

The revenue from carbon pricing in the US could amount to trillions of dollars over a ten-year period. The scenarios shown here assume that the policy cuts the quantity of fossil-fuel use by 5.22 percent per year, the rate that yields an 80 percent reduction from the initial level after thirty years.
- **Scenario 1** assumes that the carbon price initially is set at $50/mt CO_2, after which it rises at 5 percent a year.
- **Scenario 2** assumes that fossil-fuel prices rise at 8.66 percent a year (that is, the price elasticity of demand remains constant at −0.6).

in thirty years), fossil-fuel prices would rise at 8.66 percent per year (an elasticity of −0.6). In this case, the carbon price reaches $485/mt CO_2 in the tenth year, pushing gasoline prices above $6 per gallon in today's money. The cumulative carbon rent in the policy's first decade would exceed $8 trillion, an average of about $2,400 per person per year.

The actual amount of carbon rent that will result from a target-based carbon price cannot be known with certainty in advance. It could be less or more than shown in these scenarios, depending above all on the pace of technological changes in energy efficiency and alternative energy sources. But the numbers in table 3 provide some idea of the orders of magnitude we can expect.

Connecting the dots

The consequences of cutting the supply of fossil fuels can be distilled into four simple connections:

- *When supply goes down, prices go up.* Past experience suggests that the percentage increase in fuel prices will be higher than the percentage decrease in quantity.
- *When the price of fossil fuels goes up, this is passed through to consumers.* The correlation between producer prices and consumer prices is not perfect. There is some evidence that consumer prices rise more quickly in response to increases in crude oil price than they fall in response to

decreases. This is sometimes called the "rockets and feathers" phenomenon: consumer prices rise like a rocket but fall like a feather.[5] But, in any case, the correlation is tight – and here we are talking about the rocket side of the picture.

- *When fossil fuel prices rise, richer consumers pay more than poorer consumers.* The amount a household pays depends on how much it consumes. In general, the richest households have the biggest carbon footprints for the simple reason that they consume more of just about everything, including fossil fuels and things that use fossil fuels in their production and distribution.
- *But poorer consumers often pay more than richer consumers as a percentage of their incomes.* On its own, in other words, carbon pricing is akin to a regressive tax, one that hits the poor harder than the rich as a share of household income.[6] In low-income countries, the poor may consume so little fossil fuel that carbon pricing would have a progressive impact, hitting the rich harder than the poor as a percentage of income, but even in these countries rising fuel prices can pose an onerous burden on low-income households.[7]

These effects occur regardless of the cause of the reduction in fossil-fuel supplies or its motivation.

What is Carbon Rent?

If oil producers restrict supply to punish political adversaries or to raise profit margins, the end result is higher prices for consumers. If some countries were to "just say no" to fossil-fuel production, the result would be the same. If carbon pricing is implemented by means of a cap or a tax, we get the same result. The connections among the economic dots are simple and inexorable.

The crucial difference is where the carbon rent goes. In the case of the "just say no" strategy for keeping fossil fuels in the ground, as in the case of a producers' cartel, the money goes to fossil-fuel producers in proportion to the amount they continue to produce. In the case of carbon pricing, however, there are other options. One option, discussed in the next chapter, is to return the money directly to the people.

The difference between abatement costs and carbon rent

Testifying before the Senate Committee on Environment and Public Works in July 2009, the US energy secretary, Steven Chu, assured his audience that the nation could readily afford to meet the emission targets in the cap-and-trade bill then

What is Carbon Rent?

Table 4: Three ways to cut the supply of fossil fuels

Strategy	Motive	Effect
Supply restriction by cartel	Market manipulation	Higher profits for producers
Just say no	Climate stabilization	Higher profits for producers
Carbon pricing	Climate stabilization	Decided by policy design

There is more than one way to skin the fossil-fuel cat. A supply restriction imposed by a producer cartel such as OPEC, a "just say no" strategy of keeping fossils in the ground, and a carbon pricing policy would all raise the price of fossil fuels. They differ in motives (market manipulation versus climate stabilization) and effects (higher profits for producers versus other options, including carbon dividends).

before Congress. It could be done, he claimed, at a cost per household that would be "about the price of a postage stamp per day."[8] The *New York Times* columnist Paul Krugman echoed this comforting thought. "In 2020 the bill would cost the average family only $160 a year, or 0.2 percent of income," he told his readers. "That's roughly the cost of a postage stamp a day."[9]

On the other side of the political aisle, however, Congressman Mike Pence declared that the cap-and-trade bill would be "the largest tax increase in American history." His opposition was shared by all of his fellow Republicans in the House of Representatives. "By imposing a tax on every American who drives a car or flips on a light switch," thundered Speaker John Boehner, "this plan will drive up the prices for food, gasoline and electricity."[10] The *Wall Street Journal* sided with the opponents. "Americans should know," the editors warned, "that those Members who vote for this climate bill are voting for what is likely to be the biggest tax in American history."[11]

Imploring the Senate to pass the legislation in his weekly radio address to the nation, President Obama countered that "it is paid for by the polluters who currently release dangerous carbon emissions." He, too, averred that "in a decade the price to the average American will be just about a postage stamp a day."[12]

Listening to these claims and counterclaims, the average American could be forgiven for thinking that the two sides were talking about entirely different things. In a way, they were. The bill's proponents were talking about the cost of reducing emissions, or what economists term "abatement cost." This is what it costs to cut emissions – the cost, for example, of installing solar panels or more energy-efficient light bulbs. The opponents were talking instead about the extra money that consumers would have to pay for emissions that are *not* reduced. The two are not the same. In the cap-and-trade debate, however, the difference was clouded by misunderstanding, disingenuity, or both.

The postage-stamp number came from a study by the Congressional Budget Office which estimated that the cost of meeting the bill's emissions reduction targets – by investing in energy efficiency and alternative energy – would amount to about $22 billion a year in 2020, equivalent to about 18 cents per person per day.[13] This modest cost reflected the fact that the bill's targets for emission reductions started slowly, coupled with the expectation that consumers faced with rising fuel prices would choose low-cost ways to cut back.

This is depicted in figure 3a. The cost of reducing CO_2 emissions by an additional ton – referred to by economists as the "marginal abatement cost" (MAC) – rises as emissions are cut further. Initially, abatement costs are small; indeed, some steps, like turning off the lights when leaving an empty room, can save money, equivalent to a below-zero cost. But the cost of reducing emissions rises as the low-hanging fruit is picked.

The precise position of the MAC curve is uncertain, especially when we move to higher levels of emissions reduction. The curve shifts downward over time as innovations lower the costs of clean

What is Carbon Rent?

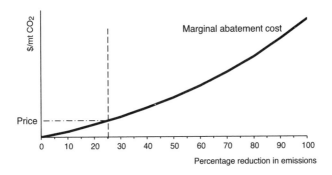

Figure 3 Target-based carbon pricing

(a) If we cut the amount of fossil carbon entering the economy by 25 percent, users are compelled to reduce ("abate") their consumption of fossil fuels. There are less expensive and more expensive ways to do this, and naturally they choose the lower-hanging fruit – the less expensive ways – first. The marginal abatement cost – the cost of reducing emissions by an additional ton – gradually rises as the least expensive options are depleted. The marginal cost at this level of abatement is the carbon price incorporated into the prices of fossil fuels, since beyond that point it is cheaper to pay the carbon price than to abate more.

energy technologies such as wind power, solar power, and battery storage. This is one reason why, as discussed in chapter 2, it is preferable to set the quantity of emissions and let the carbon price adjust rather than vice versa. No matter how rapidly costs change, however, some ways to cut emissions will be less expensive than others, and

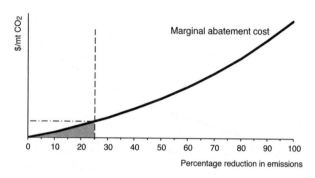

Figure 3 Target-based carbon pricing (cont.)

(b) **The total abatement cost** is the shaded area under the marginal abatement cost (MAC) curve. It is the cost of reducing emissions multiplied by the quantity of emissions reduced. Examples of abatement costs include investments in insulation or more energy-efficient appliances, switching to alternative energy, or simply bothering to turn out the lights when not in a room. If some abatement measures save money for the individuals who adopt them, the MAC curve would start below zero on the vertical axis – at a negative marginal cost – and total abatement cost would be even smaller than shown in the shaded area.

the lower-cost options typically will be chosen first.

When the supply of fossil fuels is cut by 25 percent, the corresponding MAC shown in the figure is the carbon price. This tells us how much fossil-fuel prices will rise in proportion to their carbon content. Up to that level, it is cheaper for consumers

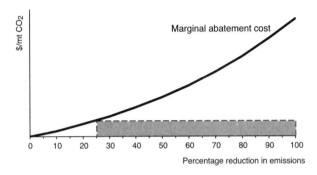

Figure 3 Target-based carbon pricing (cont.)

(c) **Carbon rent** is the money paid for emissions that are *not* reduced. It is the carbon price multiplied by the quantity of emissions. This money is not spent on energy efficiency investments, alternative energy or other abatement costs. It is the extra paid for fossil fuels, above and beyond the normal costs of production and profit margins. In economic terms, it is a *transfer*, not a resource cost.

to cut their use of fossil fuels than to pay the higher price. Beyond it, it is cheaper for them to pay the higher price than to cut fossil-fuel use further.

The total amount spent to reduce emissions is shown by the shaded triangular area in figure 3b. This is the cost of installing insulation in buildings, buying energy-efficient appliances, switching to alternative energy, and so on. This is what the proponents of the cap-and-trade bill were referring to when they compared its cost to that of a postage stamp.

What is Carbon Rent?

There is an additional cost to consumers, however, in the higher prices they pay for the fossil fuels they still consume. This cost is shown by the shaded rectangle in figure 3c. Although real enough to consumers, it is not a cost to society in the sense of a payment for more goods or services. It is a transfer, a payment for which nothing additional is received. The money simply changes hands. This is what the Republicans were talking about when they decried the bill as a hidden tax. The claim that it would have been the biggest tax hike in American history was political hyperbole, but the transfer rectangle is considerably bigger than the postage-stamp triangle, as can be seen in the figure.

The rectangle is the carbon rent. Rent is a payment for use of a scarce resource, in this case for use of the limited capacity of the biosphere to absorb CO_2 emissions. The word "tax" implies that the transfer is from individuals to governments. This is one possible use of the carbon rent, but not the only one.

Who pays?

Republican critics of the cap-and-trade bill were right about who would pay the carbon rent: consumers. Just because the carbon price is levied at the point where firms bring fossil fuels into the economy doesn't mean the buck stops there. The carbon price is incorporated into the cost of fossil fuels, passed along first to other firms who use them, and in the end to the consumers of goods and services. In this sense, private firms do not pay the carbon price: their customers do.[14]

President Obama's claim that the price would be paid by "polluters" was accurate only if one interprets this to mean paid by consumers. In this sense, I am a polluter when I eat a tomato that was produced using diesel-fueled machines and delivered to the grocery store in a diesel-fueled truck. The companies that produced and sold diesel to the farmer and the trucker are not polluters, nor are the farmer and the trucker. Instead, the "polluter" is the end-use consumer.

It is important to recognize that households are not the only final consumers. In the US, households account for about two-thirds of total fossil-fuel use. Governments at the local, state, and federal level account for another quarter, while the remainder comes from non-profit institutions.[15] These other users would also pay more as a result of the carbon price, contributing to the carbon rent.

The cost to any individual household depends

on its carbon footprint – its total consumption of fossil fuels, both direct (for example, gasoline) and indirect (for example, the fuel that was used in producing food or clothing). Richer households tend to consume more than poorer households, and therefore they would pay more carbon rent.

Figure 4 shows the distribution of carbon consumption across US households. The top one-fifth ranked by income account for almost half of total household carbon use, twice as much as the next fifth and twelve times more than the bottom fifth. With carbon pricing, their contributions to the carbon rent vary accordingly.

As a percentage of income, however, lower-income households in the US generally would pay more than richer households. This is depicted in figure 5, which shows the impact of a $100/mt price on CO_2 emissions. For households in the bottom fifth, the price would be equivalent to almost 6 percent of their incomes. For the top fifth, it would be equivalent to about 4 percent. These percentages would rise or fall with a higher or lower carbon price, but the pattern across income classes would remain the same.

The net effect of a carbon pricing policy depends not only on who pays but also on who receives the carbon rent. If most or all of the money is recycled

What is Carbon Rent?

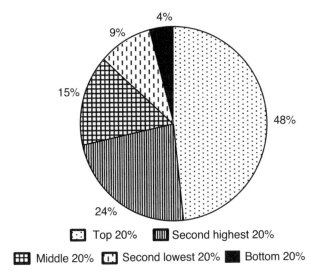

Figure 4 Carbon consumption by income class in the United States
Upper-income households consume more fossil carbon than others, for the simple reason that they consume more of just about everything. Direct energy consumption accounts for about 60 percent of household carbon footprints in the US; indirect consumption via fossil fuels used to produce and distribute other goods and services accounts for the rest.

Source: Author's calculations based on Anders Fremstad and Mark Paul, "Disrupting the dirty economy: a progressive case for a carbon dividend," People's Policy Project, September 2018.

to the public as equal dividends per person, the distributional outcome turns progressive: the poor see a net *increase* in their incomes and the purchasing power of the middle class is protected, while

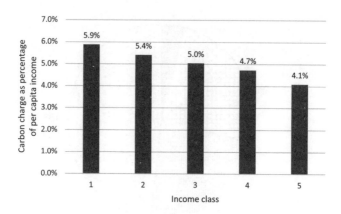

Figure 5 Impact on households of a $100/ton CO_2 price in the United States
A carbon price is regressive in the US and other industrialized countries: as a percentage of income, the poor pay more than the rich. In figure 5, each bar represents one-fifth of the population, ranked from poorest (#1) to richest (#5).

Note: Calculations are based on current consumption patterns without taking into account changes in response to carbon pricing.

Source: Author's calculations based on Anders Fremstad and Mark Paul, "Disrupting the dirty economy: a progressive case for a carbon dividend," People's Policy Project, September 2018.

as a result of their outsized carbon footprints the rich pay more than they get back. The next chapter describes how this policy would work.

4

The Carbon Dividend

In 1946, an ex-Marine pilot by the name of Jay Hammond homesteaded in the small community of Naknek, Alaska, on the windswept shore of the Bering Sea, near the world's best fishing grounds for sockeye salmon. On arrival, he was struck by the stark contrast between the wealth scooped up by commercial fishing fleets coming from elsewhere and the poverty of the local residents, who lived in "communities that were little more than rural slums," lacking such basic amenities as plumbing, electricity, telephone service, police, health care, or a high school.[1]

By the early 1960s, having been elected as a Republican state legislator, Hammond proposed a remedy to the "rip-off and run" syndrome he encountered in Naknek: allow local governments to collect a tax on every fish harvested in their waters and use the money to pay cash dividends to local residents. This would lift their incomes and, in so doing, strengthen the tax base for local government to provide public services. His effort faltered, but when Hammond was elected as Alaska's governor in 1974 he applied the same idea to an even bigger natural asset, the newly discovered oil in Alaska's North Slope, and extended it statewide. This time he succeeded.

The result was the Alaska Permanent Fund. Since the early 1980s, it has invested the state's oil royalties, and it has paid annual dividends of as much as $2,000 to every resident of the state. Not surprisingly, it has proven to be highly popular among Alaskans. The Permanent Fund also has won accolades across the political spectrum. On the left, it has been lauded as a "true socialist miracle."[2] On the libertarian right, Nobel laureate Vernon Smith has extolled it as "a model governments all over the world would be well-advised to copy."[3]

Hammond himself saw the Permanent Fund model as neither public nor private property in the usual senses of these terms. Unlike public property, the right to the oil revenue does not belong to the state. It belongs to the people. Unlike private property, this right cannot be bought and sold, or owned by corporations, or concentrated in a few hands.

The Carbon Dividend

"That money and the resources it comes from belong to *all* Alaskans, not to government or to a few 'J. R. Ewings,'" Hammond declared, referring to the fictional oil baron in the popular TV series *Dallas*, "who in states like Texas own almost all the oil."[4]

The distinctive form of property created by the Alaska Permanent Fund deserves a name of its own. I call it *universal property*. It is common property owned in equal measure by all members of the society. Universal property is individual, perfectly egalitarian, and inalienable.

Carbon dividends as universal property

In 2001, in a pioneering book called *Who Owns the Sky?*, the social entrepreneur Peter Barnes advanced a novel proposal: Why not treat the atmosphere's limited capacity to absorb carbon emissions as universal property, too? Barnes argued that we all share common assets such as air, water, and forests and have a responsibility to safeguard them:

These gifts are valuable, perhaps even priceless. They're valuable for basic biological reasons – we can't live without them – and they're also valuable in an economic sense … This wealth is the basis for all we hold dear, including life itself. Even if we never see a penny in cash, we must preserve and protect it for creatures yet unborn.

But that's not my point in this book. My point, without belittling the previous one, is that we can and *should* turn some of our shared inheritance into cash. This can be done by (1) charging market prices for using our inherited assets, and (2) paying dividends to ourselves as their rightful inheritors. We should do this not out of greed, but out of concern for protecting these assets and passing them on, undiminished, to future generations.[5]

Jay Hammond agreed that the principle behind the Permanent Fund could be extended to other natural resources.[6] Obvious candidates in Alaska included minerals and timber as well as fish. Hammond was intrigued by the proposal to apply the same idea to carbon emissions. Starting from the premise that "all citizens own a piece of the sky and should be compensated by those who pollute it," he wrote, the country could cap CO_2 emissions, auction the rights to pollute beneath the cap, and disperse some of the proceeds as "dividends to all citizen owners." The realm of universal property would be extended to Nature as a sink for disposal of wastes as well as a source of raw materials. "Pie in the sky?" Hammond mused. "Perhaps, but provocative."[7]

The Carbon Dividend

The source and sink functions of Nature are both valuable. And both are vulnerable to overuse and abuse. As universal property, however, there is an important difference between them. The Permanent Fund creates a financial incentive for Alaskans to want to pump more oil: the more that's extracted, the bigger the dividend. Carbon dividends, in contrast, arise from keeping fossil fuels in the ground. As long as the carbon price rises faster than the supply falls, a scenario consistent with past experience, as we saw in chapter 3, ratcheting down the cap leads to bigger and bigger dividends. The resulting incentive for everyone whose carbon dividends exceed what they pay in higher fossil-fuel prices is to keep even more fossil fuel in the ground. As this chapter shows, when enough of the carbon rent is returned to the public as dividends, the policy's net winners comprise a substantial majority of voters.

Before turning to details, it is useful to consider the difference between selling use rights and privatization. Alaska's oil reserves are held by the state on behalf of its people and leased to corporations that pay for the privilege of accessing them. Privatization would mean selling off the reserves rather than charging for each barrel of oil that is extracted from them. It is like the difference between selling a highway and charging a toll to drive on it.

Free-market libertarians, wedded to an ideological faith in the virtue of private enterprise and the perfidy of government, would rather sell the goose than its golden eggs. In this spirit, the economist Vernon Smith has advocated privatizing America's interstate highways, investing the proceeds, and using the earnings to pay annual dividends to all Americans.[8] One problem with such a proposal is that there can be no guarantee that the price paid for a public asset will adequately reflect its value. Indeed, the motive for private buyers would lie precisely in the prospect of driving a wedge between the two. Nor can we be confident that private owners will put long-term stewardship of the asset ahead of short-term greed.

Carbon pricing is not privatization of the atmosphere; it is the sale of use rights. The price is charged *per ton* of carbon dioxide, just as Alaska charges for each barrel of oil. Instituting a carbon price does not sell the underlying natural asset – the atmosphere's limited capacity to absorb CO_2 emissions – any more than charging a toll sells the highway. It simply means that use of the asset isn't free.

Carbon dividends are not the only possible use for carbon rent. When a cap-and-trade system hands out free permits, the private corporations that receive the permits can pocket the rent. If permits instead are auctioned (or a carbon tax is levied) and the proceeds are retained by the government, the carbon rent becomes public property in the usual sense. Only when the carbon rent is distributed as equal dividends directly to all can it be called universal property.

If one must squeeze new ideas into old labels, the best fit for universal property may be "libertarian socialism." Universal property is libertarian in its respect for the individual and socialist in its commitment to equality. As a philosophy, libertarian socialism has enough name recognition to have its own Wikipedia entry, where Noam Chomsky is cited as one of its best-known contemporary exponents.[9] The terms "libertarian" and "socialist" are often applied to opposite ends of the political spectrum, but there are undoubtedly mutually reinforcing effects between the egalitarian distribution of power and the egalitarian distribution of wealth, which are central to liberty and socialism, respectively. Carbon dividends are consistent with both.

How would carbon dividends work?

Carbon dividends are equal payments per person funded by the rent from carbon pricing. As discussed in chapter 3, carbon rent ultimately comes from the consumers of fossil fuels and of everything made and distributed by using them. Consumers pay the price even if it is initially charged at the ports, pipeline terminals, and mines where the fossil fuels enter the economy. Because each person receives the same dividend, regardless of the size of their own carbon footprint, carbon dividends do not dilute the incentive to economize on fossil fuels in response to the carbon price. Those who consume relatively little come out ahead, paying less into the carbon rent pie than they get back as dividends. Heavy consumers of fossil fuels pay more than they receive. But all have an incentive to conserve.

The principle behind carbon dividends is straightforward. The amount that each person pays is based on his or her use of a limited resource: the atmospheric space for carbon emissions. The amount that each receives is based on common ownership of the resource. From each according to use, to each according to equal ownership.

Recall the analogy to an office building where more people work than can park their cars in the lot. Fees are charged to ration the parking spaces, and the money is rebated equally to all who work in the building. Regardless of whether one cycles or takes public transport to work, or carpools or drives alone, everyone gets the same rebate. The fee is based on the individual's use of the scarce resource; the rebate is based on its common ownership. Carbon dividends apply the same principle to the atmospheric parking lot for carbon dioxide.

The logistics of dividend payments are straightforward. Like other recurrent federal payments to individuals, including Social Security and veteran's benefits, the money could be deposited electronically into individual bank accounts every month or quarter. Alternatively, each person could be issued a carbon dividend card that is linked, like a bankcard, to an account from which cash can be withdrawn at ATM machines. Those who prefer old-school technologies can receive the proverbial check in the mail.[10] As in Alaska, where residents can sign up for Permanent Fund dividends by filling out a one-page online form, signing up to receive carbon dividends would be a simple matter.[11] Front-loading the first payment, by timing it to arrive when or before fuel prices go up, would further relieve the pain for consumers and allay doubts on the part of any skeptics that the promised dividends will really materialize.

The administrative costs of a carbon price-and-dividend system would be small. The cost of collecting carbon rent in an upstream system is expected to be less than 0.25 percent of the revenue.[12] The cost of distributing dividends would be modest, too. The Permanent Fund Division of Alaska's Department of Revenue has fewer than a hundred employees and operates at an annual cost of $12 per dividend recipient, an amount that state officials expect to reduce with more automated systems.[13]

Carbon dividends would be a kind of universal basic income (UBI), but with a distinctive twist: the source of the income is a universal basic asset.[14] Much as private assets generate income for their owners in the forms of interest, dividends, and rent, universal basic assets would generate income for their owners – that is, for everyone. As a source of UBI, universal assets have advantages over redistributive taxation, among them the fact that the income rests on an inalienable property right rather than the shaky ground of budgetary politics. By providing universal income from universal property, carbon dividends would help to level the economic playing field.[15]

Winners and losers

The primary rationale for a price-and-dividend system is to keep fossil fuels where they belong:

in the ground. In the long run, this protects current and future generations from worse climate disruption. In the short run, it benefits communities that suffer from polluted air, as well as coastal and other areas already feeling the early effects of climate destabilization. The clean energy transition will also bring economic benefits in the forms of technological change, infrastructure investment, and job creation. Workers and communities that depended on the fossil-fuel industry can and should be protected by just transition policies to make sure that these gains do not come at a cost to others who can ill afford it.

The governments and corporations that claim ownership of fossil-fuel reserves will not be happy about any policy that strands their assets underground. Their more farsighted leaders may seek to reposition for the clean energy transition, but others will try to delay the day of reckoning as long as they can. This is the main political obstacle to serious climate policies.

A distinctive feature of the price-and-dividend policy is that it creates winners and losers in a more immediate sense, too: in pocketbook terms. The impact of higher fossil-fuel prices on household budgets will be highly visible. Gasoline prices, for instance, are announced in foot-high numbers on

The Carbon Dividend

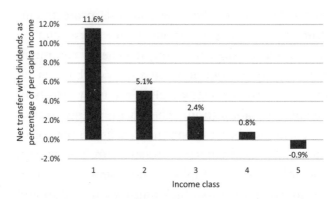

Figure 6 Net incidence of $100/ton CO_2 price coupled with dividends in the United States
Carbon prices coupled with dividends benefit the majority of people, including low-income households and the middle class. Their carbon dividends exceed what they pay as a result of higher fossil-fuel prices created by carbon pricing. The most affluent households pay more than they receive – but they can afford it. Each bar in figure 6 represents one-fifth of the population, ranked from poorest (#1) to richest (#5).

Note: Based on distribution of 100 percent of total carbon rent as dividends.

Source: Author's calculations based on Anders Fremstad and Mark Paul, "Disrupting the dirty economy: a progressive case for a carbon dividend," People's Policy Project, September 2018.

street corners across the land. Dividends will be highly visible, too, making the benefit side of the equation transparent.

As we saw in chapter 3, the carbon footprints

of lower-income households generally are smaller than those of upper-income households, for the simple reason that they do not consume as much. Hence they pay less as a result of higher fossil-fuel prices. Figure 6 shows the net effect of a price-and-dividend policy across income classes in the US, with a carbon price of $100/mt CO_2 and 100 percent of the carbon rent returned as dividends. The poorest one-fifth of households see a net gain equivalent to more than 10 percent of their incomes. The middle three-fifths come out ahead by smaller amounts. Only the top fifth experience a net loss, equivalent to about 1 percent of their incomes. They will feel the pinch, but they can afford it.

The majority of households – and hence the majority of voters – would come out ahead mon-etarily in a price-and-dividend policy, without even counting the benefits of a stable climate, clean air, and green growth. Politically, this is a compelling argument in its favor.

How do relatively small losses at the top of the income pyramid yield big gains at the bottom? Two things contribute to this outcome. The first reason is that household income in the US, as in many countries, is highly skewed to the top. A haircut on the incomes of the top fifth looks like a lot of money to everyone else. The second reason is that governments use fossil fuels, too. When all the carbon rent is disbursed as dividends, what governments pay due to higher fuel prices goes back to households, in a kind of taxation in reverse. This raises the question of whether and how to protect the purchasing power of governments, to which I return in a moment.

To reiterate a point made previously: the total amount of carbon rent cannot be known with great certainty in advance. It will depend on how rapidly technological and institutional change lowers the cost of reducing emissions. This will affect the size of the monetary impacts shown in figure 6, but not their distribution. The pattern of net gains for the majority and net losses for the highest-income stratum will persist, regardless.

The fact that carbon permits are auctioned (or, equivalently, a carbon tax is levied) in a price-and-dividend system means that there is no need for permit trading. Firms simply buy the number of permits they need (or pay the tax), corresponding to the amount of fossil carbon they bring into the economy. Unlike cap-and-trade programs, there is no leakage of carbon rent into trading profits and no scope for speculative activities.

Carbon pricing could put firms that use fossil fuels at a competitive disadvantage vis-à-vis producers in locations without a comparable carbon price. In practice, this is a significant issue only for the relatively small number of traded goods that use a great deal of fossil fuel in their production, the most important being aluminum, cement, and refined petroleum. To address this issue, and to prevent "carbon leakage," whereby emissions are relocated elsewhere in response to climate policy in a single jurisdiction, one option is to levy a carbon tariff on energy-intensive goods imported from places without comparable policies.[16] If carbon pricing is implemented at a sub-national level (by individual states in the US, for example), so tariffs are impracticable, another option is to rebate some of the carbon revenue to eligible firms.[17]

Keeping governments whole

Some carbon rent originates in purchases of fossil fuels by governments for everything from fighting wars to heating schoolrooms. In the US, federal government spending (led by defense) accounts for about 4 percent of the country's CO_2 emissions, and spending by state and local governments accounts for another 12 percent.[18]

To keep governments whole, a commensurate

fraction of carbon revenue would have to flow back to them. This can be accomplished either by treating dividends as taxable income or by retaining a fraction of the carbon revenue for government while distributing the rest as tax-free dividends.

A variant of the latter strategy featured in the first national carbon dividend legislation proposed in the US, a bipartisan bill introduced in 2009 by Senators Maria Cantwell (Democrat, Washington state) and Susan Collins (Republican, Maine). Cantwell and Collins proposed to cap emissions, auction permits under the cap, return 75 percent of the money to the public as dividends, and put 25 percent into a trust fund for government spending.[19] One attraction of the Cantwell–Collins approach is that it provides some scope for directing carbon revenues to specific public purposes. In their bill, these included transitional adjustment assistance for workers and communities, research and development in clean energy and fuels, climate change adaptation, and international projects to reduce greenhouse gas emissions. A drawback is that any reduction from dividends is equivalent to a head tax, in that it takes the same dollar amount from everyone's income, regardless of whether they are rich or poor. If dividends instead are taxed as income (and income tax rates are progressive), the rich return more to the government than do the poor.

In either case, revenue-sharing mechanisms are needed to distribute carbon revenue to state and local governments in order to keep them whole, too, in the face of rising fossil-fuel prices. As in the case of dividends to individuals, this should be done in a way that does not undermine the incentives for governments to curtail their own use of fossil fuels.

Are carbon dividends politically viable?

In 2010, when the US Senate last considered climate legislation, I participated in a conference call with leaders of environmental organizations who were discussing strategy. Some of them supported the Waxman–Markey bill, a cap-and-trade proposal backed by the Democratic leadership and passed by the House; others, including myself, favored the cap-and-dividend bill proposed by Senators Cantwell and Collins.

The cap-and-trade bill would have initially handed over much of the carbon rent as windfall profits to corporations in the form of free permits.[20] When I cautioned that the public, hit by rising fuel prices, could be unhappy about this, the bill's supporters responded that permit giveaways were necessary to protect the interests of the fossil-fuel industry, whose lobbyists otherwise would block the legislation.

"What about protecting the interests of American people?" I asked.

"On Capitol Hill, it doesn't matter what the people want," a cap-and-trade proponent responded, with the tone of an insider patiently explaining the facts of political life. "What matters is what the lobbyists want."

"Let us assume a democracy," I replied. This provoked great laughter from others on the call.

In the end, the cap-and-trade bill died in the Senate. The fossil-fuel lobbyists, it turns out, had a Plan A as well as a Plan B. Plan B was a cap-and-trade climate bill that would give them windfall profits. Plan A was no legislation at all. For many of them, A was the preferred option – and it prevailed.[21]

The argument that what really counts in the corridors of power are the wishes of the powerful, not of the people, cannot be brushed aside lightly. In a study on alternative theories of democracy, the political scientists Martin Gilens and Benjamin Page reach the following conclusion: "When the preferences of economic elites and the stands of organized interest groups are controlled for, the preferences of the average American appear to have only a minuscule, near-zero, statistically non-significant impact upon public policy."[22] In a similar vein, Yascha Mounk, a lecturer on government at Harvard, dismisses the idea that the views of ordinary people are decisive as a quaint notion that "we teach our children in civics classes."[23]

But it was not lobbyists or economic elites who won women the right to vote a century ago. It was not lobbyists or economic elites who brought us the Social Security Act in 1935, the Civil Rights Act in 1964, Medicare in 1965, or the creation of the Environmental Protection Agency in 1970. These historic achievements rose above the routines of business-as-usual politics. They were fruits of wide and deep popular mobilizations to demand action from our leaders. Something similar is required to win an effective climate policy.

A growing constituency today supports carbon dividends. The cap-and-dividend proposal of Peter Barnes was endorsed in a 2009 editorial in the mass circulation magazine *Scientific American*.[24] James Hansen, former director of NASA's Goddard Institute for Space Studies, is a prominent proponent of a fee-and-dividend policy.[25] The Citizens' Climate Lobby, a grassroots advocacy group, has taken up the proposal, generating tens of thousands of letters to members of Congress.[26] In Canada, Prime Minister Justin Trudeau announced in 2018 that carbon dividends will be introduced in all provinces that do not already have their own carbon tax, including Ontario, home to nearly two-fifths of the country's population.[27]

The sweet spot

Some politicians would prefer to put carbon revenues to other uses, but they do not agree on what those other uses should be. Conservatives tend to favor using the money to trim budget deficits or cut corporate income taxes. Liberals tend to favor using it for public spending, limiting compensation for consumers to low-income households. Underlying these contrasting preferences are divergent views on the appropriate size of government.

Among economists, a favored option is to use carbon revenue to finance cuts in the payroll taxes that fund Social Security. In the models of supply-side economics, this would add to GDP by boosting take-home pay and motivating people to work more. But the extent to which this would happen in the real world, where excess labor supply (i.e., unemployment) is common, is far from evident. The policy would leave out those who do not pay the taxes, including the elderly, the disabled, and the unemployed. The tax cut would be less transparent in recycling carbon revenues than dividends and therefore less likely to be effective in sustaining durable public support for carbon pricing.[28] Moreover, it would tie the future of Social Security to a revenue source that ultimately will dwindle when the clean energy transition nears completion.

For conservatives and liberals alike, dividends may be preferable to the uses for carbon revenue that are favored by the other side. A price-and-dividend policy neither expands the government's fiscal footprint nor shrinks it, sidestepping debates on big versus small government. The opposing sides may still disagree on other elements of climate policy, such as the need for regulations and public investment to accompany carbon pricing. But a price-and-dividend system may turn out to be the sweet spot that defines the space for political compromise and bipartisan agreement.

In the US, the prospects for national climate policy were put on hold by the election of Donald Trump in 2016, but we can hope and expect that this setback will prove to be only temporary. The connection between carbon emissions and climate disruption is all too real, and it is becoming ever more evident. At the end of the day, reality trumps wishful thinking and head-in-the-sand denial.

Taking a longer view, we can see hopeful trends. Cap-and-dividend bills were first introduced in Washington in 2009 by Congressman (now Senator) Christopher Van Hollen (Democrat, Maryland) and by Senators Cantwell and Collins. Van Hollen proposed to return 100 percent of the carbon revenue as dividends; Cantwell and Collins, as mentioned above, proposed to return 75 percent. An updated version of the Van Hollen bill has now secured 29 co-sponsors in the House of Representatives, all of them Democrats.[29]

In 2017, carbon dividends won support from a new and somewhat unexpected quarter when an organization called the Climate Leadership Council (CLC) was launched with the mission "to promote a carbon dividends framework as the most cost-effective, equitable and politically-viable climate solution."[30] Its founding document, *The Conservative Case for Carbon Dividends*, counted among its co-authors Republican elder statesmen James Baker and George Shultz and Harvard economists Martin Feldstein and Gregory Mankiw (who chaired the President's Council of Economic

Advisers under Ronald Reagan and George W. Bush, respectively).[31]

The CLC proposal calls for a carbon tax starting at $40 per ton and increasing over time, with the proceeds returned to the public as quarterly dividends. Regulations "that are no longer necessary upon the enactment of a rising carbon tax" would be phased out. In an effort to win over the fossil-fuel lobby, the plan holds out the carrot that "robust carbon taxes would also make possible an end to federal and state tort liability for emitters," a move that would head off current and future lawsuits seeking restitution for the impacts of climate disruption. There is no necessary connection, however, between carbon pricing and liability waivers.[32]

This marked the first time that carbon dividends won significant backing on the Republican side of America's political divide. Polls show that a majority of Republicans believe that climate change is real and that reducing carbon emissions would help to combat it; their opposition to climate policies advanced by Democrats springs more from mistrust of the messenger than mistrust of the message.[33]

In June 2018, an advocacy group called Americans for Carbon Dividends, co-chaired by ex-Senators John Breaux (Democrat, Louisiana) and Trent Lott (Republican, Mississippi), was launched to support the CLC plan.[34] Senator Breaux explained his support for carbon dividends in a radio interview:

> We spent over 30 years trying other approaches and they haven't worked ... We've tried a whole bunch of different approaches, more regulations from the government to try and limit the amount of carbon we emit to the atmosphere, and so far, nothing has worked very well. And so we decided that this method of putting a fee on those who emit the carbon emissions and then returning that amount of money back to the public is a way to get both sides to come together and actually have a chance of getting something done.[35]

It remains to be seen whether these initiatives on both sides of the political aisle will bear fruit. But the door to a bipartisan carbon dividend policy appears to have opened a crack.[36]

No doubt there will still be diehard opposition from fossil-fuel interests, trying to prevent their assets from being stranded. But they've had a good run and can afford to retire with their winnings. No doubt there will still be disagreements about the need for regulation and public investment to complement carbon pricing. But these do not need to be resolved in order to agree that a price-and-dividend policy is a good place to start. No doubt there will be some in these intensely partisan times who regard any bipartisan initiative with suspicion, if not outright hostility, and some who will stick resolutely to their own preferred uses for carbon revenue rather than embracing dividends for all.

The key to overcoming these political hurdles will be broad public support for a policy that keeps fossil fuels in the ground – and does this not at the expense of ordinary people but, instead, to their benefit.

No one stands to make a killing from carbon dividends. No deep-pocket funders have an incentive to lobby for them. The people must demand them. What we need to get carbon dividends, in other words, is a democracy.

National solutions to an international problem?

But wait. Climate change is a global problem. Even if a single country or a few countries wean themselves off fossil fuels, will it matter? How can there be national solutions to an international problem?

It is true that success in combating climate change requires a clean energy transition worldwide, not only in one country or a few countries. This is the collective action problem that has bedeviled international climate negotiations: Why should any

WHICH SIDE ARE YOU ON?

CLIMATE DISRUPTION	CLIMATE STABILIZATION
DIRTY AIR	CLEAN AIR
NON-RENEWABLE ENERGY	RENEWABLE ENERGY
POLLUTER PROFITS	CARBON DIVIDENDS

Ask yourself – and ask your politicians: Which side are you on?

Graphic by Kim Weinstein.

country move to reduce its own emissions if others don't?

The here-and-now benefits of clean air, green growth, and carbon dividends offer a way out of this dilemma, providing compelling reasons for countries to curtail their use of fossil fuels regardless of what others do. As countries adopt price-and-dividend policies, these benefits will become more apparent, resulting in a demonstration effect that can inspire emulation by others. In other words, national policies can be stepping stones to international climate accords. This is not putting the cart before the horse; it's rethinking which is which.

One can imagine a price-and-dividend system at the international level, too, in which carbon revenues are distributed equally to everyone worldwide. There is no international entity, however, that could administer or enforce such a system. Moreover, the fact that it would bring net pocketbook losses for the majority of people in upper-income countries on account of their larger-than-world-average carbon footprints would cast doubt on the political feasibility of winning approval in these nations.

National price-and-dividend systems, on the other hand, would bring monetary benefits to the majority of people in every single country of the world. Coupled with the appeals of clean air and the clean energy economy, price-and-dividend policies offer a politically feasible way to keep fossil fuels in the ground. The outcome would be not only a whole that is the sum of the parts but also a sounder footing for reaching an international accord on allocation of the Earth's remaining carbon space.

The path forward

The challenges posed by climate disruption are not going to disappear. Sooner or later, countries throughout the world will abandon fossil fuels in favor of clean energy. The sooner, the better.

The same strategies that we use successfully to resolve other congestion problems, such as automobile parking, can be applied to carbon emissions. These solutions typically combine prices and rules. Just because you pay to park in the lot does not mean that you can park anywhere and everywhere; you have to park in designated spaces. Just because something is legal – just because you follow the rules – does not mean it should be free. Prices do not preclude rules, and rules do not preclude prices.

If our goal is to reduce carbon emissions, and to do so rapidly enough to meet climate-stabilization objectives such as the 1.5 to 2°C target set by the Paris Agreement, the carbon price must be target-based. Rather than setting a price and hoping for the best, we must anchor it to the target by means of a hard cap or a tax that is indexed to emissions. The two can be combined, as I have noted, by capping the number of carbon permits and letting the tax serve as the floor price for permit auctions.

How high the target-based carbon price will be cannot be predicted with precision in advance. If other policy instruments – regulations and public investments – are highly effective, the carbon price will be lower than if they are not. If technological progress rapidly lowers the cost of wind power and solar power, the carbon price will be lower than if cost-saving innovations come slowly. Extrapolating from what we know – that is, from past experience – we can expect that the carbon prices needed to meet tough emissions targets will be substantial. If so, the amount of money paid by consumers as a result of higher fossil-fuel prices will be substantial, too.

A crucial question from the standpoints of fairness and political durability is where this carbon rent will go. Rather than turning it over to private corporations or government treasuries, a price-and-dividend policy would return the money to the people. This would translate the philosophical principle that the gifts of Nature belong equally to all into a practical reality. It would treat the limited capacity of the air to absorb carbon emissions as universal property. And it would protect the majority of people – especially low-income and middle-class households – from financial hardship caused by the rising prices of fossil fuels.

The only way this will happen, however, is if the people who stand to benefit – you and me – work together to make it happen. Electing leaders who recognize the need for a clean and safe environment is only a first step. President Franklin D. Roosevelt's famous advice to the Social Security advocates who helped to elect him was "Now make me do it." The same maxim applies to climate policy.

Here is the bottom line: if you want to safeguard the Earth's climate for future generations, if you want to breathe clean air, if you want to build a green economy, and if you want carbon dividends, it is up to you to win them. The gifts of Nature may be free, but securing them for the benefit of all is not. The challenge is to make your leaders follow your lead. To make history, we must make them do it.

Frequently Asked Questions

1) How can we be certain that a carbon price will do enough to keep fossil fuels in the ground?
It's not enough to set any old price on carbon – it has to be the right price. "Right" means a price that is consistent with our targets for emission reductions.

Target-based prices can be ensured by setting the quantity of fossil carbon we allow into the economy and letting the price adjust, rather than setting the price and hoping it yields the desired results. This can be done with a cap-and-permit system, or a tax anchored to the quantity of emissions, or a combination of the two in which the tax is the floor price in permit auctions.

2) Why not just tax corporate polluters?
The simplest and most effective point at which to

charge the carbon price is where corporations bring fossil fuels into the economy. But it would be an error to think that the buck will stop there.

Whenever the supply of fossil fuels is reduced by a cap, a tax, or otherwise, their price to consumers goes up. This is a simple economic fact of life. For corporations, the carbon price is another cost of doing business, which they pass along to their customers. The buck stops with the final consumers of fossil fuels and everything that's made and distributed using them.

3) Won't consumers balk at higher fuel prices?
You bet. This is why dividends are crucial for the political durability of target-based carbon prices. Dividends would transparently and fairly protect the purchasing power of the majority of people, including low-income households and the middle class, in the face of rising fuel costs.

4) Why should Bill Gates get a share? Why not give carbon dividends only to people who really need them?
There are three strong arguments for dividends being universal rather than restricted to certain people.

Number one is the ethical premise that the gifts of Nature are universal property belonging to all. "All" means everyone: black and white, young and old, even rich and poor.

Number two is a practical consideration: means-testing or other eligibility screens would escalate the administrative costs of the program.

Number three is that universality is the key to political durability. If programs such as Social Security and Medicare in the US did not offer universal coverage, it's not evident that they would still be with us today.

Of course, Bill Gates might not think it's worth 10 minutes of his time to sign up for his dividend. That's a choice for him to make.

5) Wouldn't some low-income households be made worse off – for example, residents of rural areas who have to drive long distances?

In some cases, a reasonable argument can be made for dedicating some of the carbon revenue to extra compensation for particular locations or population subgroups. The Canadian carbon dividend policy unveiled in October 2018, for example, includes extra help for rural people who depend more heavily on fossil fuels. Ideally, such additional assistance would take the form of a dividend supplement across the board that doesn't diminish the incentive for eligible individuals to reduce their personal use of fossil fuels.

6) Wouldn't spending the money on renewable energy or energy efficiency do more to reduce fossil-fuel emissions?

Some environmentalists prefer this option. But it is important to realize that, as long as the carbon price is anchored to a hard ceiling on the amount of fossil fuels entering the economy, such spending will not result in any additional reduction in emissions. For example, if the money is used to subsidize more energy-efficient appliances, reduced emissions in the electric power sector would simply open more space under the ceiling for emissions from other sectors, such as transportation.

That said, a very good case can be made for public investments as a crucial part of the clean energy transition. Commuters, for example, can't switch from private automobiles to public transport if the latter does not exist. One possible source for funding such investments is to dedicate part of the carbon revenue for this purpose. Another is to end the subsidies that governments today lavish on fossil fuels and redirect this money to more beneficial uses, including investments in clean energy and public transportation.

7) Wouldn't it be more efficient to use carbon revenue to cut other taxes?

Some economists prefer this option, claiming that the tax cuts could boost economic growth and employment. Liberals like the idea of cutting payroll taxes; conservatives like the idea of cutting corporate income taxes. Orthodox models predict that this use of carbon revenues would have a small but positive effect on the economy. But the idea that tax cuts spur growth and employment by increasing incentives to supply labor and capital – i.e., "supply-side economics" – rests on the shaky premise that the economy already makes full use of their available supply, ignoring the all too common realities of involuntary unemployment, underemployment, and underutilized capital. In fact, by putting money into the pockets of working people, carbon dividends would stimulate the economy by increasing demand.

8) If we give the money to the people, won't they spend more on fossil fuels?

Carbon dividends are the people's money and they can do what they want with it. If some want to spend it on fossil fuels, they're free to do so. But they will pay a higher price for their fossil-fuel habits and will have an incentive to cut back. And as long as the carbon price is firmly anchored to hard emission-reduction targets, how they spend their money won't affect the overall quantity of emissions.

9) Would carbon prices make regulation unnecessary?

No. Prices and rules are complements, not substitutes.

It is true that some regulations could be made superfluous by effective carbon pricing. If the price is high enough to make coal unprofitable for electricity generation, for example, regulations on emissions from coal-fired plants would become superfluous – and whether or not they remain on the books would be immaterial.

But, even with an effective carbon price, smart regulations would continue to be an important part of the policy mix. Regulations are needed to address other sources of greenhouse gas emissions apart from fossil carbon, including methane. Regulations are needed to promote practices that sequester carbon, such as sustainable forest management. Smart regulations can also help to "bend the cost curve" by accelerating innovation and technological changes that lower the costs of energy efficiency and clean energy.

10) Would a carbon price guarantee less pollution in overburdened communities?

Simply putting a price on pollution – via a tax, a cap, or a combination of the two – does not guarantee that pollution will be reduced in every location. Pollution "hot spots" could persist, or even worsen, unless we also adopt policies specifically designed to eliminate this risk. Evidence from California underscores the importance of the issue: in the initial years of the state's cap-and-trade policy for carbon emissions, pollution often increased in economically and politically vulnerable communities.[1] This is another reason we need smart regulations as a complement to carbon prices.

11) Isn't pollution just wrong? Why let people pay to pollute?

A famous study found that, when Israeli day care centers began to levy a fine on parents who showed up late to pick up their children, the tardiness problem got worse rather than better. Apparently, some parents reckoned that, as long as they paid the price, arriving late was now OK.[2] Carbon pricing is different. The imposition of "sin taxes" on tobacco and alcohol does not cause people to smoke or drink more. Carbon prices do not cause people to burn more fossil fuels – in fact, they give them an obvious reason to burn less.

It's great for people to reduce their carbon footprints for ethical reasons, too. With carbon pricing, virtue is not only its own reward – it is economically beneficial as well.

12) Would carbon pricing make a country's industries less competitive in world markets?

For most companies, energy costs are much less important than their costs for labor and other materials. But this is a concern for energy-intensive trade-exposed industries such as aluminum producers, petroleum refiners, and cement manufacturers. In these cases, border carbon adjustments can help to level the playing field. Carbon tariffs can be levied on imports from countries that do not have comparable carbon prices, and carbon rebates can be provided on exports to such countries.

13) Are carbon dividends a Republican (small government) idea?

Carbon dividends appeal to Republicans who recognize the need for a clean energy transition and who understand the importance of carbon prices in moving it forward but want a "revenue-neutral" policy that does not increase the size of the government budget. Carbon dividends do not reduce the government budget, either, provided that dividends are taxed as income or some carbon revenue is set aside to keep government whole.

14) Are carbon dividends a Democratic (big government) idea?

Carbon dividends appeal to Democrats who understand the importance of carbon pricing for the clean energy transition and recognize that durable public support for increased fossil-fuel prices will require a policy that returns carbon revenue to the people fairly and transparently. By returning the money to households, a carbon price-and-dividend policy does not increase the size of the government budget.

15) Can we trust the government to pay us dividends?

In the US, some polls have reported that many people are skeptical about carbon dividends because they don't believe the government would really pay them. Outside Alaska, this novel idea may seem so radical as to be unbelievable.

Americans trust the government to pay Social

Security benefits. We trust it to pay benefits to veterans. We even trust it to put people in jail. Why not trust it to pay dividends? If Alaska's state government can do it, others can, too.

But the main guarantee is this: The only way we'll get carbon dividends in the first place is by demanding them from our leaders. If we can make them pass the law, we can make them follow it.

16) Won't fossil-fuel corporations try to make sure this never happens?

Fossil-fuel corporations can be expected to oppose any policy that keeps fossil fuels in the ground and turns "their" reserves into stranded assets. Here I put "their" in quotation marks because corporations did not create the Earth's oil, coal, and natural gas. Their claims to these resources recall what Adam Smith wrote about land in *The Wealth of Nations*: "The landlords, like all other men, love to reap where they never sowed, and demand a rent even for its natural produce."[3]

In the first decade of the twenty-first century, American politicians tried to sweeten the deal for the fossil-fuel industry by offering them windfall profits from free permits in cap-and-trade proposals. It didn't work. Today, some may offer waivers of corporate liability for climate disruption as an inducement – an indication, perhaps, of how seriously the heads of fossil-fuel corporations take this threat to their bottom lines.

Keeping fossil fuels in the ground will benefit current and future generations of humankind by protecting the climate, cleaning the air, and ushering in the clean energy economy of the future. The vast majority of the world's people will be winners. But the "owners" of fossil fuels will be losers.

There is no way around this simple fact. Some may feel sorry for the losses that fossil-fuel corporations and their stockholders will incur. But, in any market economy, some investors make good bets and others make bad ones. Those who make bad bets lose money. Betting that they can keep making profits by extracting poisonous fuels from under the ground will – I hope – turn out to be a bad bet.

Acknowledgements

I was first introduced to the idea of carbon dividends by Peter Barnes at a meeting in New York City nearly twenty years ago. At the time Peter was writing his book *Who Owns the Sky?*, where he proposed a cap-and-dividend system for carbon pricing modeled on the Alaska Permanent Fund's treatment of oil revenues. Peter is one of the rare people I've met who truly can be called a visionary. My intellectual debt to him is enormous.

I am also deeply indebted to my former doctoral student Matthew Riddle, with whom I began to study and write about the distributional impacts of carbon pricing more than a decade ago. It is a cliché to say teachers learn from their students, but in Matt's case it is quite true. I have also learned much from former University of Massachusetts Amherst doctoral students Elizabeth Stanton, Mark Paul, and Anders Fremstad.

My colleagues at the Political Economy Research Institute and Department of Economics have supported my work in ways too numerous to mention, and I am immensely grateful for their support and friendship. I have also benefited from conversations on climate policy with Frank Ackerman, Alex Barron, David Bollier, Marc Breslow, Ray Bradley, Dallas Burtraw, Michael Conroy, Steve DeCanio, Peter Dorman, Eban Goodstein, Robin Hahnel, Betsy Hartmann, Manuel Pastor, Robert Repetto, Mike Sandler, Kristen Sheeran, and Theda Skocpol. The usual caveats apply.

I also want to express my gratitude to George Owers of Polity Press for first encouraging me to write this book, two anonymous reviewers for thoughtful comments and suggestions, and Arpita Biswas, Cobi Frangillo, Tyler Hansen, and Kim Weinstein for assistance in research and preparation of the book. The Mesa Refuge in Point Reyes Station, California, provided me the perfect space to start writing it.

My greatest thanks go to my grandchildren, whose joy and beauty offer a constant reminder of why the future is worth fighting for.

Further Reading

Frank Ackerman, *Can We Afford the Future?* London: Zed Books, 2009.

Peter Barnes, *Who Owns the Sky? Our Common Assets and the Future of Capitalism.* Washington, DC: Island Press, 2001.

Peter Barnes, *With Liberty and Dividends for All.* Oakland, CA: Berrett-Koehler, 2014.

James K. Boyce, *Economics for People and the Planet: Inequality in the Era of Climate Change.* London: Anthem Press, 2019.

Dallas Burtraw and Samantha Sekar, "Two world views on carbon revenues," *Journal of Environmental Studies and Sciences* 4 (2014): 110–20.

Donald Marron and Elaine Maag, *How to Design Carbon Dividends.* Washington, DC: Tax Policy Center, Urban Institute & Brookings Institution, 2018.

Robert Pollin, *Greening the Global Economy.* Cambridge, MA: MIT Press, 2015.

Notes

Chapter 1 Why Cut Carbon?

1 Anil Ananthaswamy, "Hothouse Earth: what it was like the last time our planet warmed up," *New Scientist* 198/2661 (2008): 34–8.

2 H. J. Dowsett, M. M. Robinson, A. M. Haywood, D. J. Hill, A. M. Dolan, D. K. Stoll, W. L. Chan, A. Abe-Ouchi, M. A. Chandler, N. A. Rosenbloom, and B. L. Otto-Bliesner, "Assessing confidence in Pliocene sea surface temperatures to evaluate predictive models," *Nature Climate Change*, 2/5 (2012): 365–71.

3 S. Jevrejeva, L. P. Jackson, R. E. Riva, A. Grinsted, and J. C. Moore, "Coastal sea level rise with warming above 2C," *Proceedings of the National Academy of Sciences*, 113/47 (2016): 13342–7.

4 O. Hoegh-Guldberg, P. J. Mumby, A. J. Hooten, R. S. Steneck, P. Greenfield, E. Gomez, C. D. Harvell, P. F. Sale, A. J. Edwards, K. Caldeira, and N. Knowlton,

"Coral reefs under rapid climate change and ocean acidification," *Science*, 318/5857 (2007): 1737–42.

5 Chris Mooney, "How climate change could counterintuitively feed winter storms," *Washington Post*, January 4, 2018; National Oceanic and Atmospheric Administration (NOAA), "Climate change and extreme snow in the U.S.," www.ncdc.noaa.gov/news/climate-change-and-extreme-snow-us.

6 Caitlyn Kennedy and Rebecca Lindsey, "What's the difference between global warming and climate change?" NOAA, June 17, 2015, www.climate.gov/news-features/climate-qa/whats-difference-between-global-warming-and-climate-change.

7 Dylan Matthews, "Donald Trump has tweeted climate change skepticism 115 times. Here's all of it," *Vox*, June 1, 2017, www.vox.com/policy-and-politics/2017/6/1/15726472/trump-tweets-global-warming-paris-climate-agreement.

8 Peter Holley, "Stephen Hawking just moved up humanity's deadline for escaping Earth," *Washington Post*, May 5, 2017.

9 International Energy Agency, CO_2 *Emissions from Fossil Fuel Combustion*. Paris: IEA, 2017; Marielle Saunois et al., "The global methane budget 2000–2012," *Earth System Science Data* 8 (2016), www.earth-syst-sci-data.net/8/697/2016/.

10 US Environmental Protection Agency, *Inventory of Greenhouse Gas Emissions and Sinks: 1990–2015, Executive Summary* (2017), Table ES-2, www.epa.gov/sites/production/files/2017-02/documents/2017_executive_summary.pdf. This percentage refers to the

fossil-fuel share of gross CO_2-equivalent greenhouse gas emissions. In the US the fossil-fuel share of net emissions (including carbon reabsorption from land use, land use change, and forestry) is even higher, at 91 percent.

11 National Academy of Sciences, *Negative Emissions Technologies and Reliable Sequestration: A Research Agenda*. Washington, DC: NAS, 2018.

12 World Health Organization, *Ambient Air Pollution: A Global Assessment of Exposure and the Burden of Disease*. Geneva: WHO, 2016.

13 Organisation for Economic Co-operation and Development, *The Cost of Air Pollution: Health Impacts of Road Transport*. Paris: OECD, 2014.

14 Ibid., p. 63.

15 J. Lelieveld, S. Evans, M. Fnais, D. Giannadaki, and A. Pozzer, "The contribution of outdoor air pollution sources to premature mortality on a global scale," *Nature* 525 (2015): 367–84. (This estimate assumes carbonaceous particles to be five times more toxic than inorganic particles.)

16 Drew Shindell, "The social cost of atmospheric release," *Climatic Change* 130 (2015): 313–26.

17 K. He, Y. Lei, X. Pan, Y. Zhang, Q. Zhang, and D. Chen, "Co-benefits from energy policies in China," *Energy* 35 (2010): 4265–74; K.-M. Nam, C. J. Waugh, S. Paltsev, J. M. Reilly, and V. J. Karplus, "Carbon co-benefits of tighter SO_2 and NO_x regulations in China," *Global Environmental Change* 23 (2013): 1648–61.

18 M. M. Berk, J. C. Bollen, H. C. Eerens, A. J. G.

Manders, and D. P. van Vuuren, *Sustainable Energy: Trade-Offs and Synergies between Energy Security, Competitiveness, and Environment*. Bilthoven: Netherlands Environmental Assessment Agency, 2006.

19 Drew Shindell, Greg Faluvegi, Karl Seltzer, and Cary Shindell, "Quantified, localized health benefits of accelerated carbon dioxide emissions reductions," *Nature Climate Change* 8 (2018): 291–5.

20 The job numbers in the table assume that two-thirds of this investment goes into renewables and one-third into energy efficiency; altering the proportions between them has only a minor effect on the comparison. Details can be found in Robert Pollin et al., *Global Green Growth: Clean Energy Industrial Investments and Expanding Job Opportunities*. Vienna: United Nations Industrial Development Organization, 2015.

21 Tony Mazzocchi, "A superfund for workers," *Earth Island Journal* 9/1 (1993): 41–2.

22 Robert Pollin and Brian Callacci, "A just transition for U.S. fossil fuel industry workers," *American Prospect*, July 6, 2016.

23 For estimates of EU and global fossil-fuel subsidies, see Sarabjeet Hayer, *Fossil Fuel Subsidies*, European Parliament, Directorate General for Internal Policies, Policy Department A: Economic and Scientific Policy, March 2017, www.europarl. europa.eu/RegData/etudes/IDAN/2017/595372/IPOL _IDA(2017)595372_EN.pdf.

24 Diane Cardwell, "What's up in coal country?

Alternative-energy jobs," *New York Times*, September 30, 2017.

25 Emma Bryce, "Germany's transition from coal to renewables offers lessons for the world," *Scientific American*, September 5, 2017.

26 Todd BenDor, T. William Lester, Avery Livengood, Adam Davis, and Logan Yonavjak, "Estimating the size and impact of the ecological restoration economy," *PLoS ONE* 10/6 (2015).

27 Amory Lovins, *Small is Profitable*. Snowmass, CO: Rocky Mountain Institute, 2002.

28 Richard J. Campbell, *Weather-Related Power Outages and Electric System Resiliency*. Washington, DC: Congressional Research Service, 28 August 2012.

29 Sadie Cox, Pieter Gagnon, Sherry Stout, Owen Zinaman, Andrea Watson, and Eliza Hotchkiss, *Distributed Generation to Support Development-Focused Climate Action*. Washington. DC: US Agency for International Development and National Renewable Energy Laboratory, September 2016.

30 John W. Diamond and George R. Zodrow, *The Effects of Carbon Tax Policies on the US Economy and the Welfare of Households*. New York: Columbia SIPA Center on Global Energy Policy, July 2018.

Chapter 2 Why a Price on Carbon?

1 R. Calel and A. Dechezleprêtre, "Environmental policy and directed technological change, evidence

from the European carbon market," *Review of Economics and Statistics* 98 (2016): 173–91.

2 On the role of public investment in innovation, see Mariana Mazzucato, *The Entrepreneurial State: Debunking Public vs. Private Sector Myths.* London: Anthem Press, 2013.

3 World Bank, *State and Trends of Carbon Pricing 2017.* Washington, DC: World Bank, November 2017.

4 D. Coady, I. Parry, L. Sears, and B. Shang, "How large are global fossil fuel subsidies?" *World Development* 91 (2017): 11–27. By a broader measure that includes unpriced externalities such as climate change and dirty air, this study estimated the worldwide subsidy at $5.3 trillion a year. See also Doug Koplow, "Defining and measuring fossil fuel subsidies," in J. Skovgaard and H. van Asselt, eds, *The Politics of Fossil Fuel Subsidies and their Reform.* Cambridge: Cambridge University Press, 2018.

5 Calculated from data in World Bank, *State and Trends of Carbon Pricing 2017.*

6 J. Bosman, "Unlikely allies campaign for a gas-tax holiday," *New York Times*, May 2, 2008.

7 Alissa J. Rubin, "Macron inspects damage after 'yellow vest' protests as France weighs state of emergency," *New York Times*, December 1, 2018.

8 James K. Boyce and Raymond S. Bradley, "3.5°C in 2100?" Political Economy Research Institute, July 2018, www.peri.umass.edu/images/boycebradleyFinal_2018.pdf.

9 William D. Nordhaus and Paul Sztorc, *DICE 2013R: Introduction and User's Manual*. New Haven, CT: Cowles Foundation, 2013, p. 11.

10 Economists sometimes apply a lower "social discount rate" in assessing society-wide projects (such as climate change mitigation). Even at the 1.4 percent discount rate used in the 2007 Stern Review, the significance of long-term impacts is greatly muted; for example, $1 million in damages 200 years from now would count for only $60,000 today.

11 L. Clarke et al., "Assessing transformation pathways," in O. Edenhofer et al., eds, *Climate Change 2014: Mitigation of Climate Change. Contribution of Working Group III to the Fifth Assessment Report of the Intergovernmental Panel on Climate Change*. Cambridge: Cambridge University Press, 2014, p. 490.

12 William D. Nordhaus, "The question of global warming: an exchange," *New York Review of Books*, September 25, 2008. In recent years, Professor Nordhaus has adopted a more urgent tone. After receiving the 2018 Nobel Prize in Economics, he warned in an interview that, unless we limit warming to less than 2°C, "we're in for changes in the Earth's system that we can't begin to understand in depth." C. Davenport, "After Nobel in Economics, William Nordhaus talks about who's getting his pollution-tax ideas right," *New York Times*, October 13, 2018.

13 IPCC, *Climate Change 2014: Synthesis Report*, 2014, p. 79.

14 Robert S. Pindyck, "Climate change policy: what do the models tell us?" *Journal of Economic Literature* 51/3 (2013): 861–2.

15 SCC estimate based on a 3 percent discount rate, from Interagency Working Group on the Social Cost of Greenhouse Gases, *Technical Support Document: Technical Update of the Social Cost of Carbon for Regulatory Impact Analysis under Executive Order 12866*. Washington, DC, August 2016, p. 4. To assess the potential for "lower-probability, higher-impact outcomes from climate change, which would be particularly harmful to society," the Working Group (p. 15) recommends a 2020 SCC of $123/mt.

16 Nicholas Stern, *The Economics of Climate Change: The Stern Review*. Cambridge: Cambridge University Press, 2007.

17 Chris Mooney, "New EPA document reveals sharply lower estimate of the cost of climate change," *Washington Post*, October 11, 2017; Brad Plumer, "Trump put a low cost on carbon emissions. Here's why it matters," *New York Times*, August 23, 2018.

18 UK Department of Energy & Climate Change, *Carbon Valuation in UK Policy Appraisal: A Revised Approach*, July 2009, p. 1, https://assets.publishing. service.gov.uk/government/uploads/system/uploads/ attachment_data/file/245334/1_20090715105804_e ____carbonvaluationinukpolicyappraisal.pdf.

19 *Report of the High-Level Commission on Carbon Prices*. Washington, DC: World Bank, 29 May 2017.

20 Reto Knutti, Joeri Rogelj, Jan Sedláček, and Erich M. Fischer, "A scientific critique of the two-degree

climate change target," *Nature Geoscience* 9 (2016).

21 Carl-Friedrich Schleussner et al., "Science and policy characteristics of the Paris Agreement temperature goal," *Nature Climate Change* 6 (2016): 827–35.

22 Ambarish V. Karmalkar and Raymond S. Bradley, "Consequences of global warming of 1.5°C and 2°C for regional temperature and precipitation changes in the contiguous United States," *PLoS ONE* 12/1 (2016): 2.

23 Xavier Labandeira, José M. Labeaga, and Xiral López-Otero, "A meta-analysis on the price elasticity of energy demand," *Energy Policy* 102 (2017): 549–68.

24 Swiss Confederation, Federal Office for the Environment, *Swiss Climate Policy at a Glance*. Bern, 2014, www.bafu.admin.ch/bafu/en/home/topi cs/climate/publications-studies/publications/swiss-cl imate-policy-at-a-glance. See also M. Hafstead, G. E. Metcalf, and R. C. Williams III, "Adding quantity certainty to a carbon tax through a tax adjustment mechanism for policy pre-commitment," *Harvard Environmental Law Review* 41 (2017): 41–57.

25 Smart regulations can be a valuable complement to carbon pricing, for example, by accelerating promising lines of technological innovation. For discussion, see J. K. Boyce, "Carbon pricing: effectiveness and equity," *Ecological Economics* 150 (2018): 52–61.

26 US Congressional Budget Office, *An Evaluation of Cap-and-Trade Programs for Reducing U.S. Carbon Emissions*. Washington, DC, June 2001.

Chapter 3 What is Carbon Rent?

1 OECD, Crude oil production (indicator), doi: 10.1787/4747b431-en.

2 Food & Water Watch, "Dividend and conquer," January 2013, www.foodandwaterwatch.org/sit es/default/files/dividend_and_conquer_ib_jan_2013. pdf.

3 Michael L. Ross, "How the 1973 oil embargo saved the planet," *Foreign Affairs*, October 15, 2013.

4 This price trajectory is one of several scenarios mapped in Alexander R. Barron, Allen A. Fawcett, Marc A. C. Hafstead, James R. McFarland, and Adele C. Morris, "Policy insights from the EMF 32 study on U.S. carbon tax scenarios," *Climate Change Economics* 9 (2018).

5 Robert W. Bacon, "Rockets and feathers: the asymmetric speed of adjustment of UK retail gasoline prices to cost changes," *Energy Economics* 13/3 (1991): 211–18; M. Chesnes, "Asymmetric pass-through in U.S. gasoline prices," *Energy Journal* 37/1 (2016).

6 See, for example, A. Mathur and A. C. Morris, "Distributional effects of a carbon tax in broader U.S. fiscal reform," *Energy Policy* 66 (2014): 326–34; B. Bureau, "Distributional effects of a carbon tax on car fuels in France," *Energy Economics* 33 (2011): 121–30; Q. Wang, K. Hubacek, K. Feng, Y.-M. Wei, and Q.-M. Liang, "Distributional effects of carbon taxation," *Applied Energy* 184 (2016): 1123–31. Apart from impacts on household

expenditures, carbon pricing could have other distributional effects via price-indexed government transfer programs or other interactions, some of which may make its overall impact less regressive (J. Horowitz, J.-A. Cronin, H. Hawkins, L. Konda, and A. Yuskavage, *Methodology for Analyzing a Carbon Tax*. US Department of the Treasury, Office of Tax Analysis, Working Paper 115, January 2017). Here I focus simply on expenditures, where the effects are largest and most visible, and hence most politically salient.

7 See, for example, Mark Brenner, Matthew Riddle, and James K. Boyce, "A Chinese sky trust? Distributional impacts of carbon charges and revenue recycling in China," *Energy Policy* 35 (2005): 1771–84 (based on 1995 data from China when industrialization was at an earlier stage); Ashokankur Datta, "The incidence of fuel taxation in India," *Energy Economics* 32 (2010), Suppl.: 26–33; P. Rathore and S. Bansal, "Distributional effects of adopting carbon tax in India: an economic analysis," *Review of Market Integration* 5 (2013): 271–302.

8 Secretary Chu's statement to the Senate Committee of Environment and Public Works, Washington, DC, 7 July 2009, www.energy.gov/articles/secretary-chus-statement-senate-committee-environment-and-public-works.

9 Paul Krugman, "It's easy being green," *New York Times*, September 24, 2009.

10 NBC News, "Obama implores Senate to pass climate bill," June 27, 2009, www.nbcnews.com/

id/31565446/ns/us_news-environment/t/obama-implo
res-senate-pass-climate-bill/.

11 "The cap and tax fiction," *Wall Street Journal*, June
25, 2009.

12 CNN, "Obama says energy legislation a 'jobs bill,'"
June 27, 2009, http://politicalticker.blogs.cnn.
com/2009/06/27/obama-says-energy-legislation-a-jo
bs-bill/.

13 Congressional Budget Office, "Estimated costs to
households from the cap-and-trade provisions of
H.R. 2454," 19 June 2009.

14 This is not to say, of course, that firms are unaf-
fected. Sales of fossil fuels would decline – that is the
basic aim of carbon pricing – and some firms (e.g.,
coal producers) could go out of business. But firms
would not be "paying the carbon price" in the sense
of spending on fossil fuels that cannot be recouped
from their customers.

15 James K. Boyce and Matthew E. Riddle, *Keeping
the Government Whole*. Political Economy Research
Institute, Working Paper no. 188, November 2008,
www.peri.umass.edu/publication/item/290-keeping-
the-government-whole-the-impact-of-a-cap-and-divi
dend-policy-for-curbing-global-warming-on-govern
ment-revenue-and-expenditure.

Chapter 4 The Carbon Dividend

1 Jay Hammond, *Tales of Alaska's Bush Rat Governor*.
Kenmore, WA: Epicenter Press, 1994, pp. 148–50.

2 Dylan Matthews, "The amazing true socialist

miracle of the Alaska Permanent Fund," *Vox*, February 13, 2018, www.vox.com/policy-and-pol itics/2018/2/13/16997188/alaska-basic-income-perm anent-fund-oil-revenue-study.

3 Sean Butler, "Life, liberty and a little bit of cash," *Dissent*, Summer 2005, pp. 41–7.

4 Hammond, *Tales of Alaska's Bush Rat Governor*, p. 256.

5 Peter Barnes, *Who Owns the Sky? Our Common Assets and the Future of Capitalism*. Washington, DC: Island Press, 2001.

6 Hammond, *Tales of Alaska's Bush Rat Governor*, p. 323.

7 Jay Hammond, *Chips from the Chopping Block*. Kenmore, WA: Epicenter Press, 2001, p. 140.

8 Vernon Smith, "Trump's best deal ever: privatize the interstates," *Wall Street Journal*, June 28, 2017.

9 "Libertarian socialism," https://en.wikipedia.org/wiki/Libertarian_socialism#Contemporary_libertar ian_socialism. See also Noam Chomsky, "The Soviet Union versus socialism," *Our Generation*, Spring/Summer 1986, https://chomsky.info/1986/.

10 Allen H. Lerman, *Paying Dividends to American Residents from Carbon Fee Revenue*. Coronado, CA: Citizens' Climate Education, 2018, https://11 bup83sxdss1xze1i3lpol4-wpengine.netdna-ssl.com /wp-content/uploads/2018/06/AHLerman.v10a.05 2418.F1-1.pdf. For more on dividend logistics, see Donald Marron and Elaine Maag, *How to Design Carbon Dividends*. Washington, DC: Tax Policy Center, Urban Institute & Brookings Institution,

December 12, 2018, https://www.taxpolicycenter. org/publications/how-design-carbon-dividends/full.

11 The Alaska Permanent Fund form for adults can be accessed at https://pfd.alaska.gov/LinkClick.asp x?fileticket=2R4LPj55Xgs%3d&portalid=6&tim estamp=1531759968793; the version for children can be accessed at https://pfd.alaska.gov/LinkClick. aspx?fileticket=1Vzbjt_F5vg%3d&portalid=6&time stamp=1531760056188.

12 S. Smulders and H. Volleberg, "Green taxes and administrative costs," in C. Carraro and G. Metcalf, eds, *Behavioral and Distributional Effects of Climate Policy*. Chicago: University of Chicago Press, 2001.

13 Gregg Erikson and Cliff Groh, "How the APF and PFD operate," in K. Widerquist and M. W. Howard, eds, *Alaska's Permanent Fund Dividend: Examining its Suitability as a Model*. New York: Palgrave Macmillan, 2012.

14 James K. Boyce and Peter Barnes, "$200 a month for everyone?" *TripleCrisis*, November 7, 2016, http:// triplecrisis.com/200-a-month-for-everyone/. See also Michael W. Howard, "A cap on carbon and a basic income," in K. Widerquist and M. W. Howard, eds, *Exporting the Alaska Model: Adapting the Permanent Fund Dividend for Reform around the World*. New York: Palgrave Macmillan, 2012.

15 On UBI, see Annie Lowrey, *Give People Money: How a Universal Basic Income Would End Poverty, Revolutionize Work, and Remake the World*. New York: Crown, 2018.

16 Christoph Böhringer, Edward J. Balistreri, and Thomas F.Rutherford, "The role of border carbon adjustment in unilateral climate policy," *Energy Economics* 34 (2012), Suppl. 2: S97–S110.

17 In Massachusetts, for example, proposed carbon pricing legislation would rebate part of the carbon revenue to employers, based on the number of their employees. Commonwealth of Massachusetts, "An Act Combating Climate Change," Senate Bill 1821, filed January 19, 2017, https://malegislature.gov/Bills/190/SD1021.

18 James K. Boyce and Matthew E. Riddle, *Keeping the Government Whole*. Political Economy Research Institute, Working Paper no. 188, November 2008, www.peri.umass.edu/publication/item/290-keeping-the-government-whole-the-impact-of-a-cap-and-divi dend-policy-for-curbing-global-warming-on-govern ment-revenue-and-expenditure.

19 J. K. Boyce and M. E. Riddle, *CLEAR Economics: State-Level Impacts of the Carbon Limits and Energy for America's Renewal Act*. Political Economy Research Institute, July 2011, www.peri.umass.edu/publication/item/363-clear-economics-state-level-im pacts-of-the-carbon-limits-and-energy-for-america-s-renewal-act-on-family-incomes-and-jobs.

20 The 2009 Waxman–Markey bill also provided for some permits to be auctioned, with the share of auctioned permits rising in later years and equal per capita dividends to be paid from some of the auction revenue starting in the year 2026.

21 For an insightful post-mortem on cap-and-trade, see

Theda Skocpol, *Naming the Problem: What it Will Take to Counter Extremism and Engage Americans in the Fight against Global Warming*. Prepared for the Symposium on the Politics of America's Fight against Global Warming, Harvard University, February 14, 2012, https://scholars.org/sites/schol ars/files/skocpol_captrade_report_january_2013_0. pdf.

22 Martin Gilens and Benjamin I. Page, "Testing theories of American politics: elites, interest groups, and average citizens," *Perspectives on Politics* 12 (2014): 575.

23 Yascha Mounk, "America is not a democracy," *The Atlantic*, March 2018, p. 82.

24 "Act now on global warming," *Scientific American*, July 2009. See also the Chesapeake Climate Action Network at http://climateandprosperity.org/res ources/.

25 James E. Hansen, "The imperative of a carbon fee and dividend," in L. Bernard and W. Semmler, eds, *The Oxford Handbook of the Macroeconomics of Global Warming*. Oxford: Oxford University Press, 2014.

26 More on CCL can be accessed at http://citizenscli matelobby.org/.

27 Shawn McCarthy, "Ottawa to announce rebates in provinces without carbon tax," *Globe and Mail*, October 22, 2018.

28 The economist Nicholas Stern and his colleagues have come to a similar conclusion, arguing that "traditional economic lessons on efficiency and equity

are subsidiary to the primary challenge of garnering greater political acceptability" and that dividends "are more stable over time, particularly in countries that are bogged down with issues of economic inequality, political distrust and polarization." The latter seems to be a fair description of much of the world. See David Klenert, Linus Mattauch, Emmanuel Combet, Ottmar Edenhofer, Cameron Hepburn, Ryan Rafaty, and Nicholas Stern, "Making carbon pricing work for citizens," *Nature Climate Change* 8 (2018): 669–77.

29 "Van Hollen, Beyer, introduce cap and dividend legislation," press release, office of Congressman Don Beyer, January 29, 2018, https://beyer.house.gov/news/documentsingle.aspx?DocumentID=735. See also Mike Sandler, "Cap and dividend bill introduced in U.S. Senate," http://www.feasta.org/2018/03/01/cap-and-dividend-bill-introduced-in-u-s-senate-a-ray-of-hope-regardless-of-its-political-feasibility/.

30 CLC's mission statement can be accessed at www.clcouncil.org/mission/.

31 James A. Baker III, Martin Feldstein, Ted Halstead, N. Gregory Mankiw, Henry M. Paulson, Jr., George P. Schultz, Thomas Stephenson, and Rob Walton, *The Conservative Case for Carbon Dividends*, February 2017, www.clcouncil.org/media/TheConservativeCaseforCarbonDividends.pdf.

32 Lee Wasserman and David Kaiser, "Beware of oil companies bearing gifts," *New York Times*, July 25, 2018. Several major corporations, including ExxonMobil, BP, and Royal Dutch Shell, have voiced

support for the CLC plan. An ExxonMobil spokesman denied that the liability release component of the plan was part of the firm's decision to endorse it. John Schwartz, "Exxon Mobil lends its support to a carbon tax proposal," *New York Times*, June 20, 2017.

33 L. Van Boven, P. J. Ehret, and D. K. Sherman, "Psychological barriers to bipartisan public support for climate policy," *Perspectives on Psychological Science* 13 (2018): 492–507.

34 More on AFCD can be accessed at www.afcd.org/the-solution.

35 National Public Radio, "Living on Earth," July 6, 2018, https://loe.org/shows/shows.html?programID=18-P13-00027.

36 Another opening came in November 2018 as this book was going to press: three Democratic and two Republican Congressmen introduced the Energy Innovation and Carbon Dividend Act, a bill that would levy a carbon fee and return 100 percent of the revenue to the public as taxable dividends. For details, see Noah Kaufman, "How the bipartisan Energy Innovation and Carbon Dividend Act compares to other carbon tax proposals," Columbia SIPA Center on Global Energy Policy, November 27, 2018.

Frequently Asked Questions

1 Lara Cushing, Dan Blaustein-Rejto, Madeline Wander, Manuel Pastor, James Sadd, Allen Zhu,

and Rachel Morello-Frosch, "Carbon trading, co-pollutants, and environmental equity: evidence from California's cap-and-trade program (2011–2015)," *PLoS Medicine* 15/7 (2018): e1002604; James K. Boyce and Michael Ash, "Carbon pricing, co-pollutants, and climate policy: evidence from California," *PLoS Medicine* 15/7 (2018): e1002610.

2 Uri Gneezy and Aldo Rustichini, "A fine is a price," *Journal of Legal Studies* 29 (2000): 1–17.

3 Adam Smith, *The Wealth of Nations*, Book 1, chapter 6.